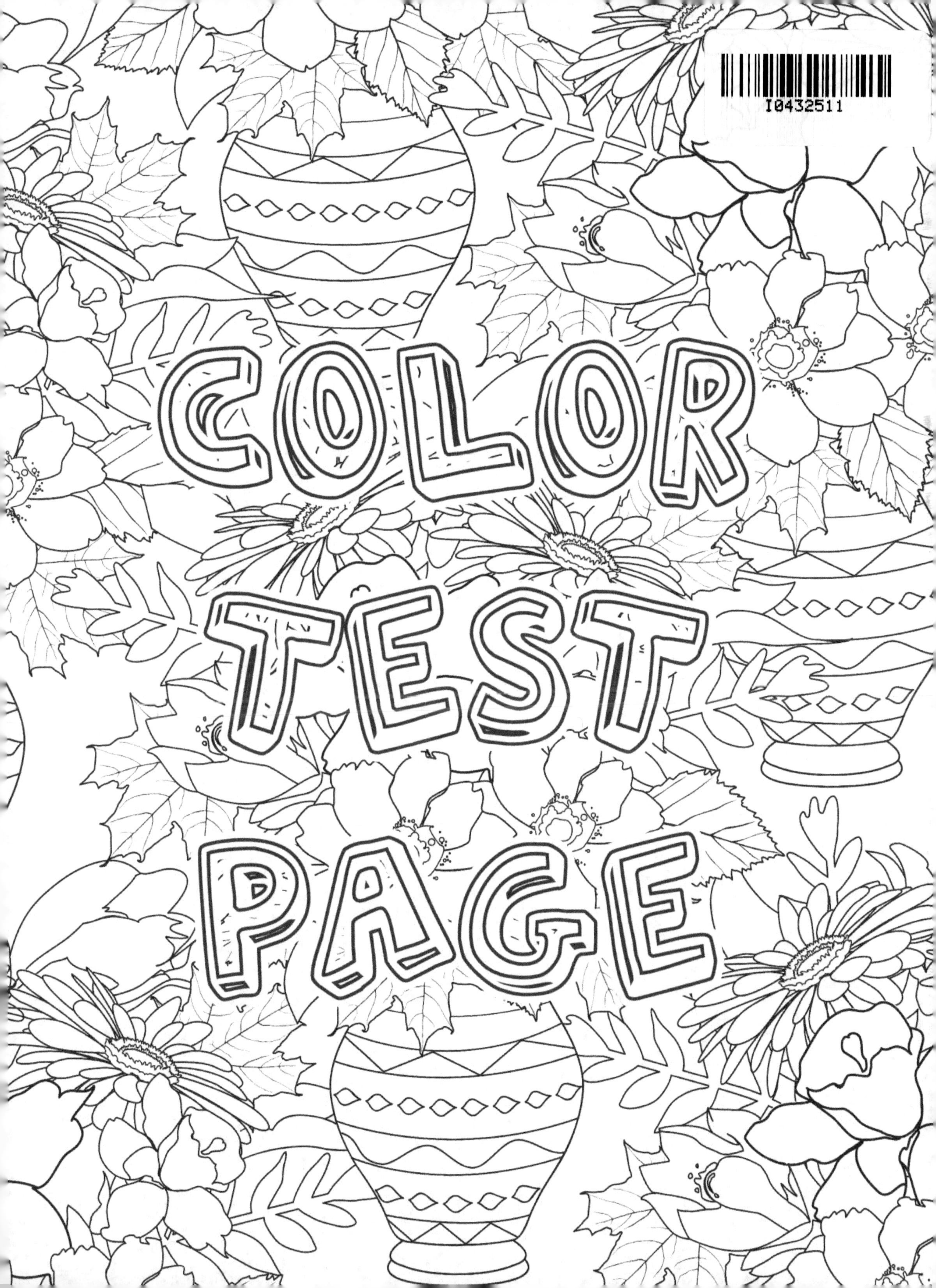
COLOR
TEST
PAGE

GRATITUDE MANDALA

ADUTL COLORING BOOK

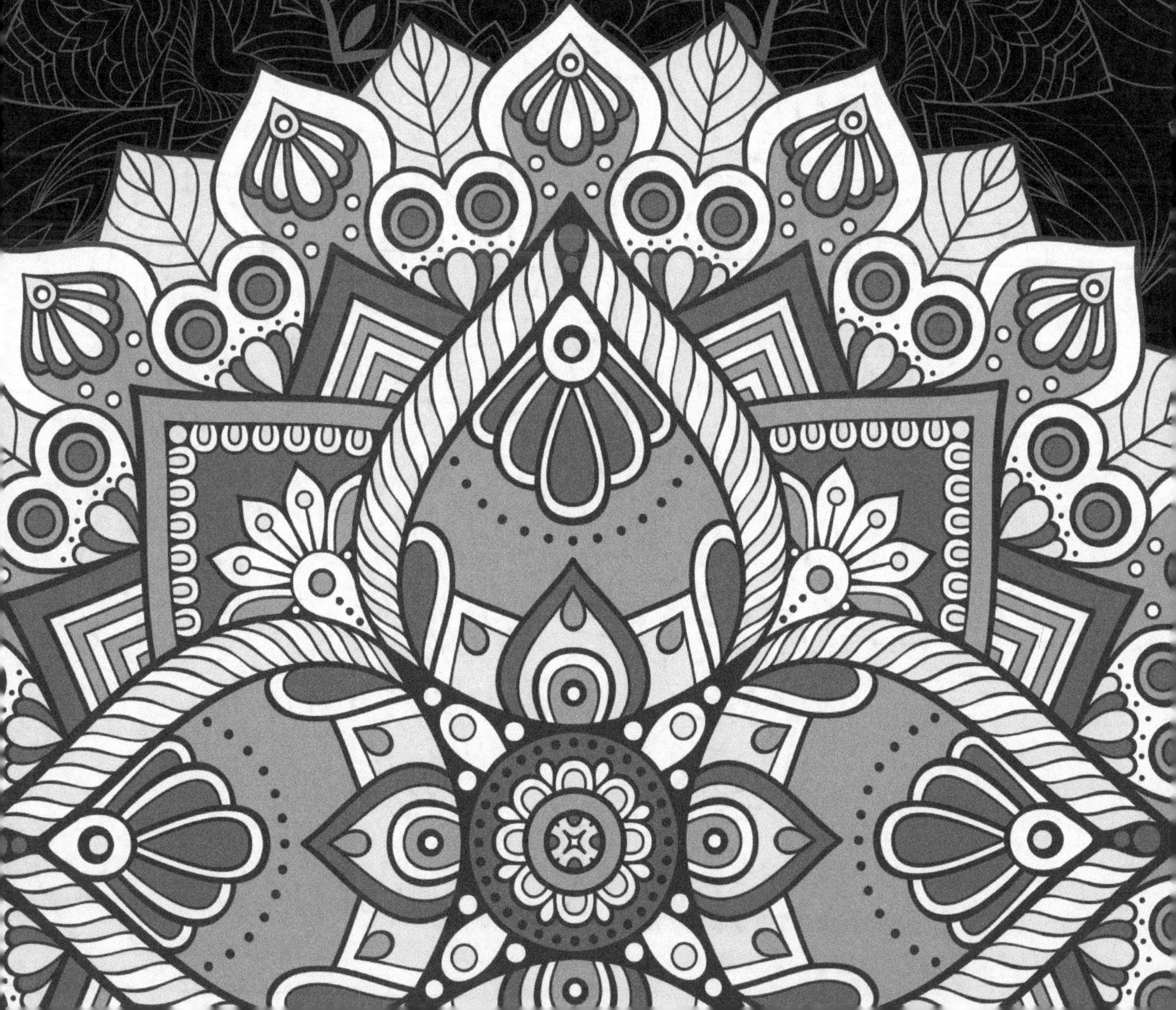

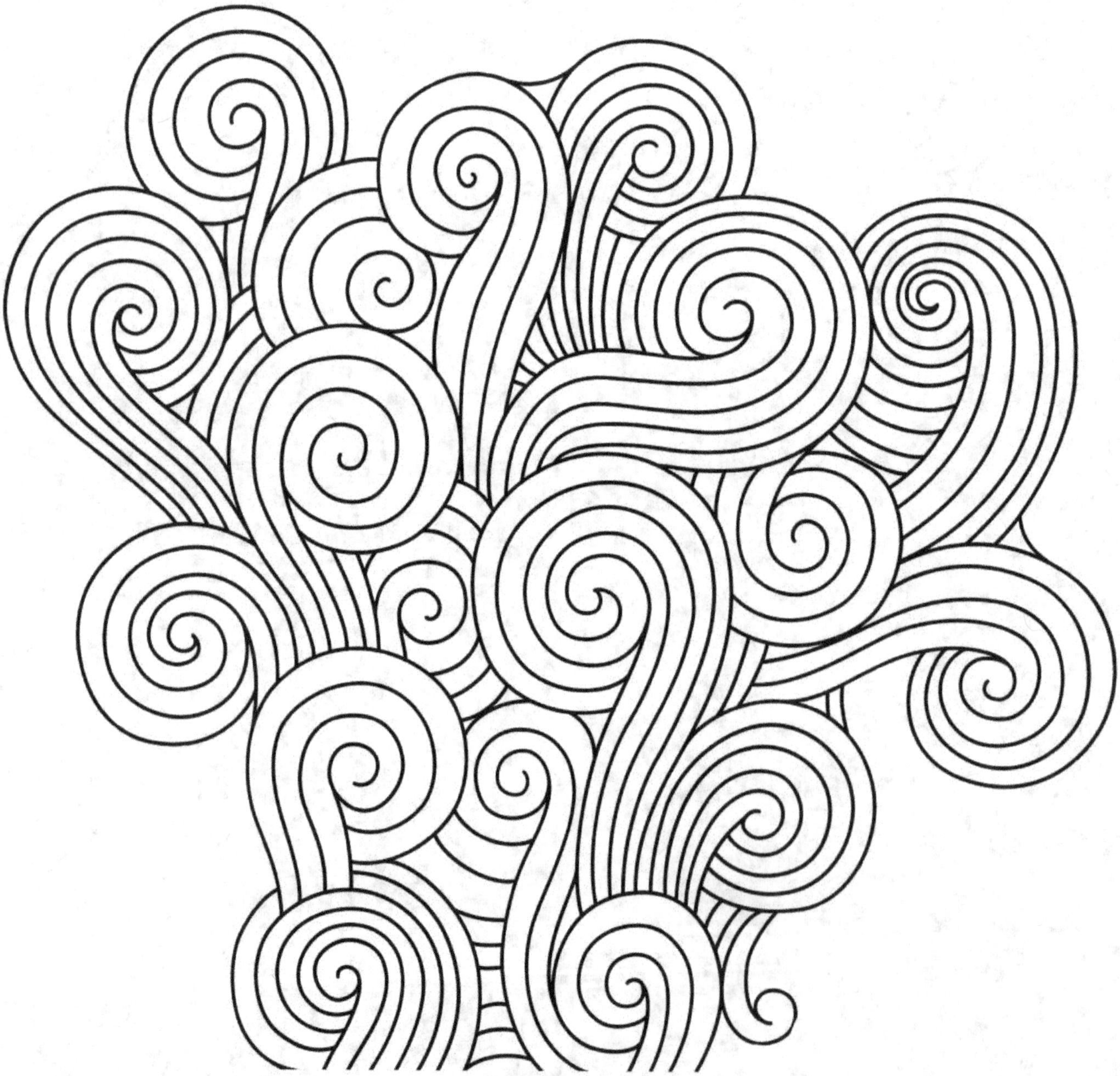

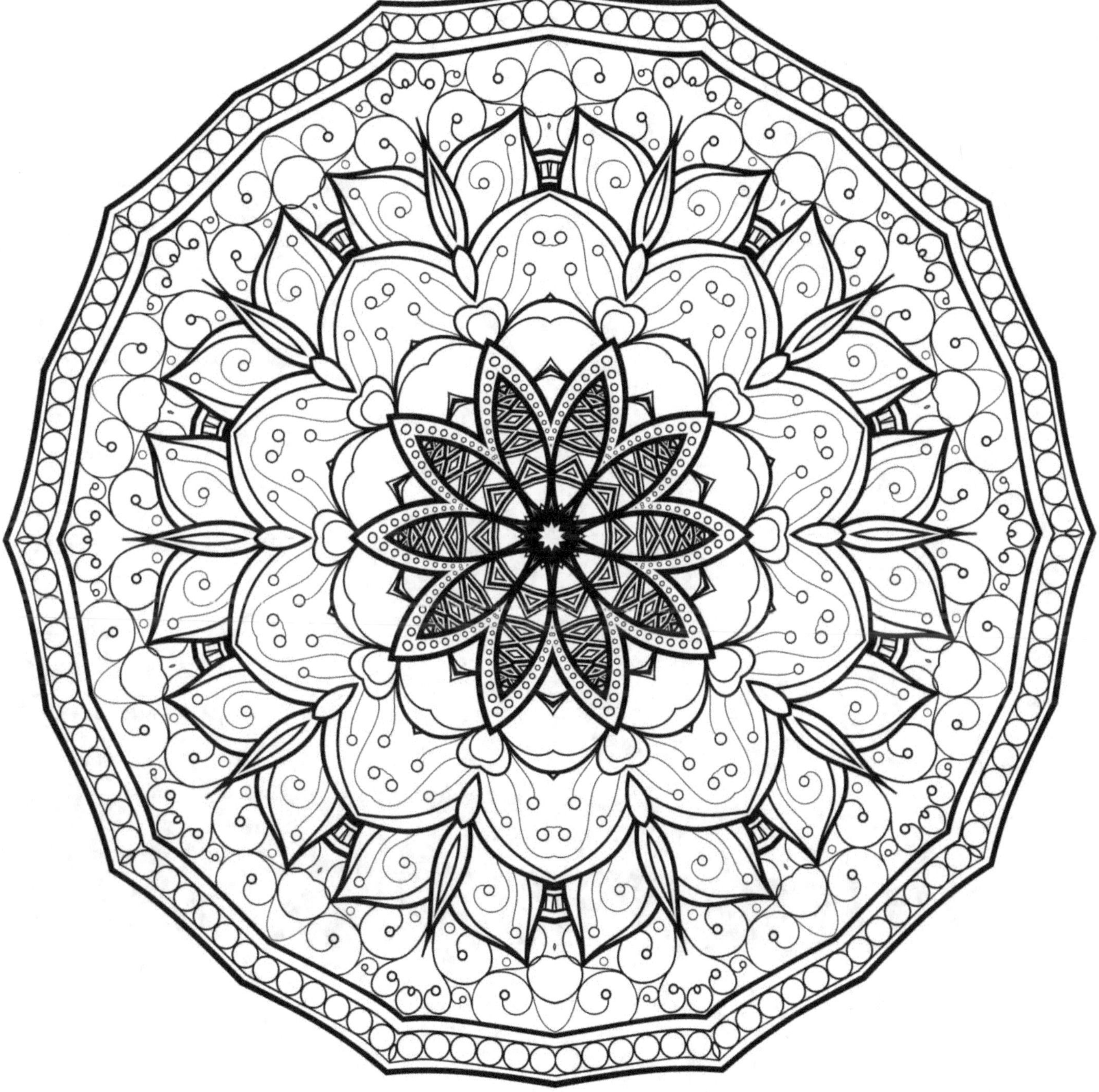

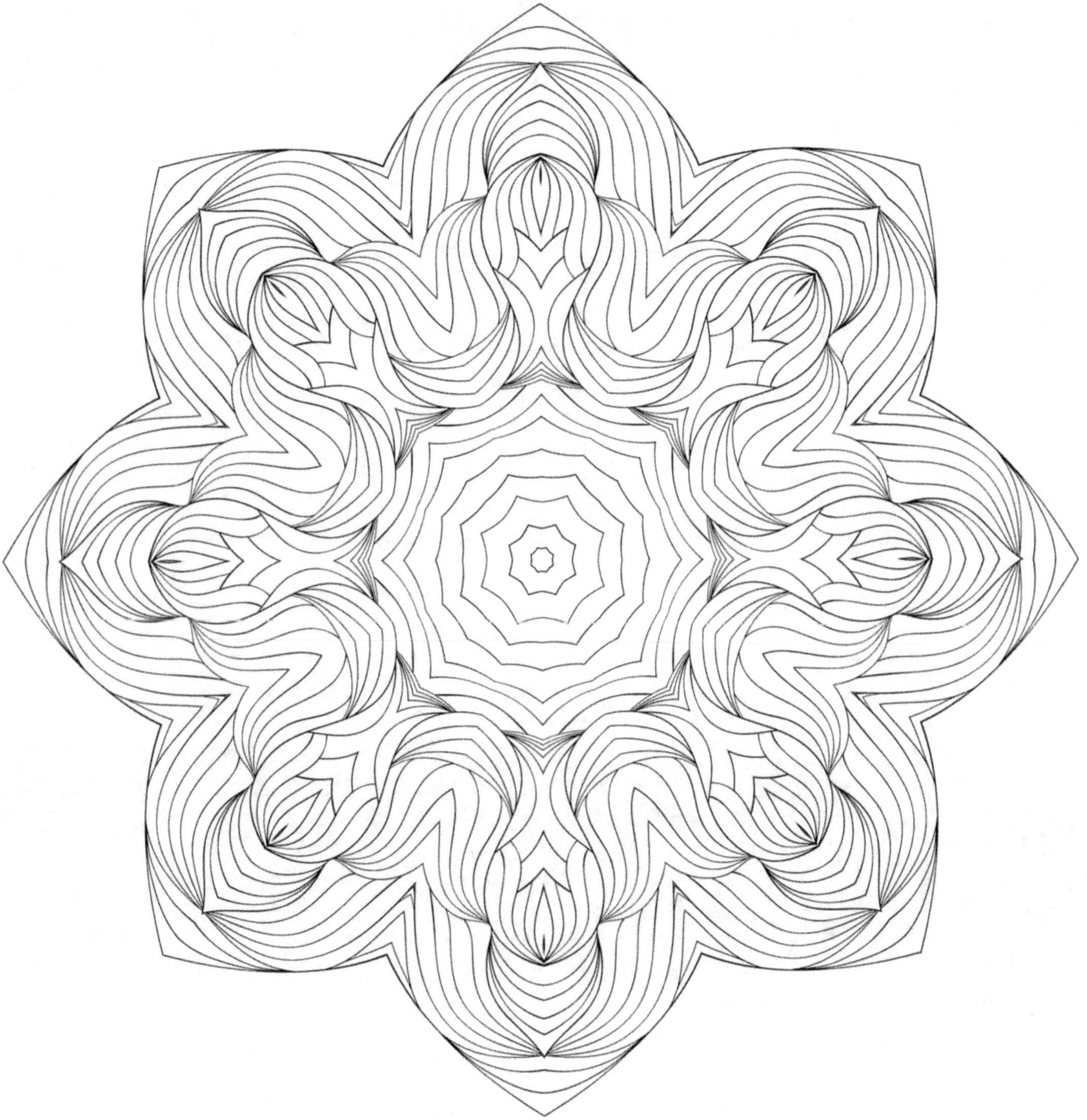

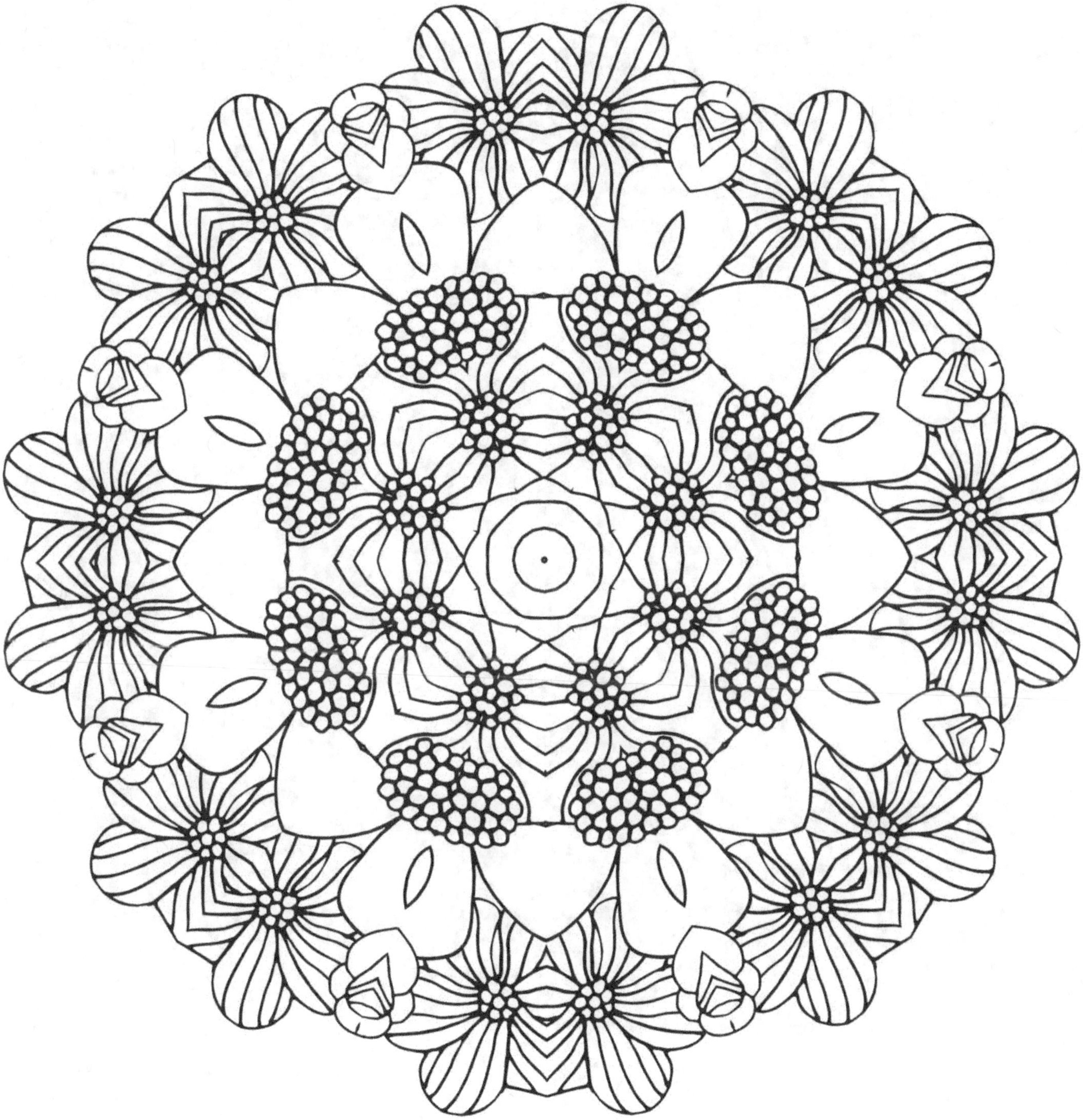

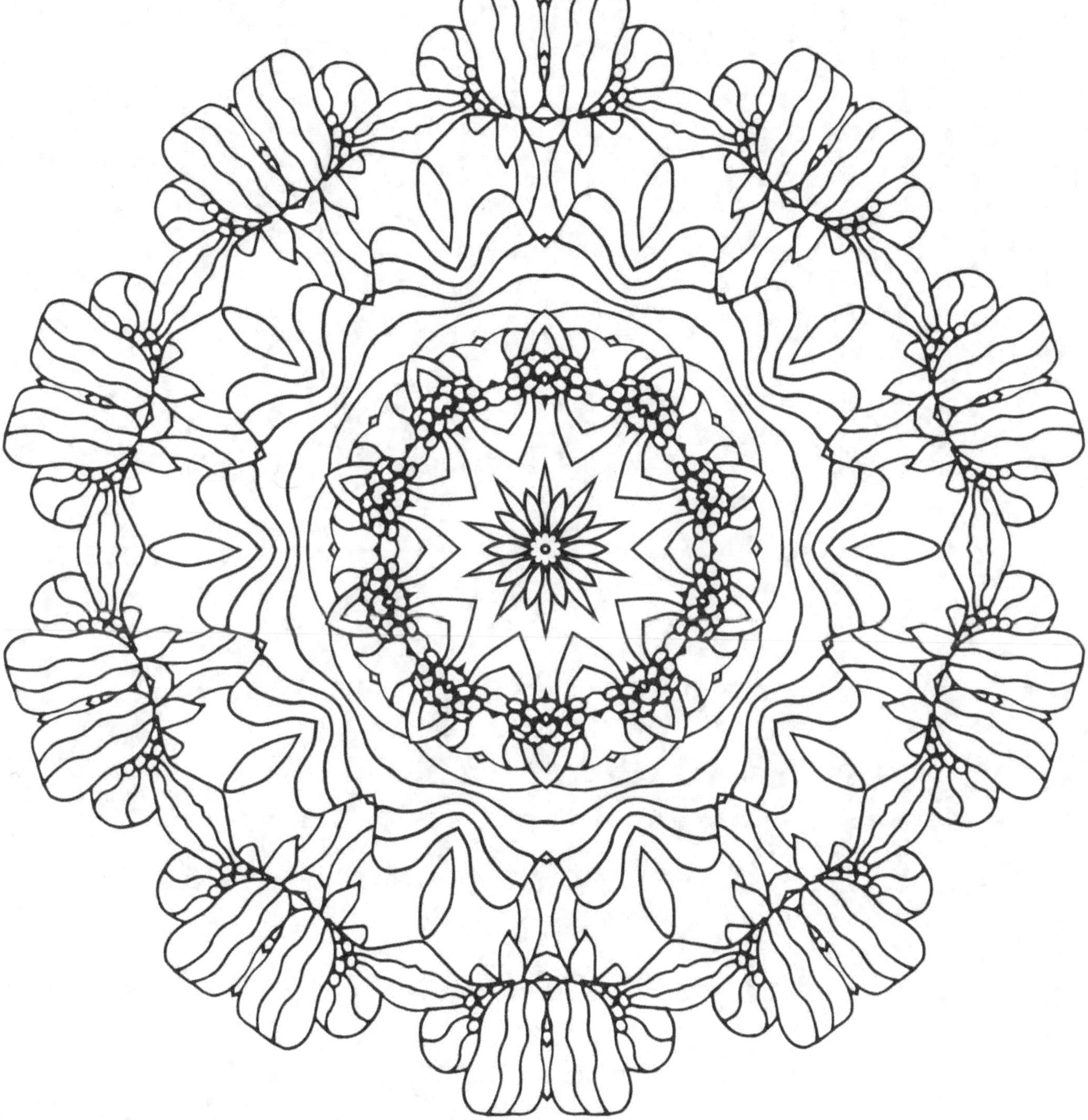

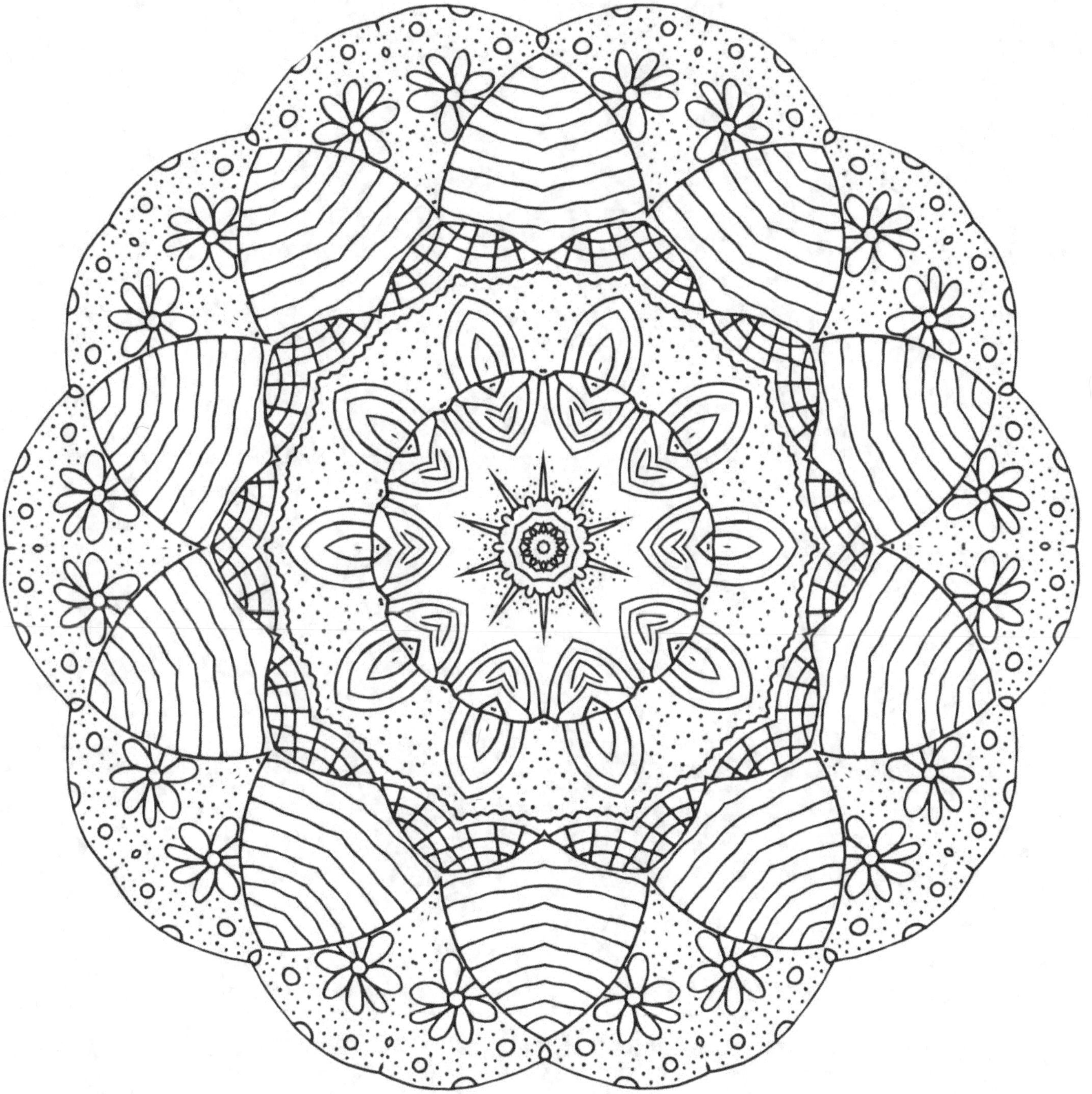

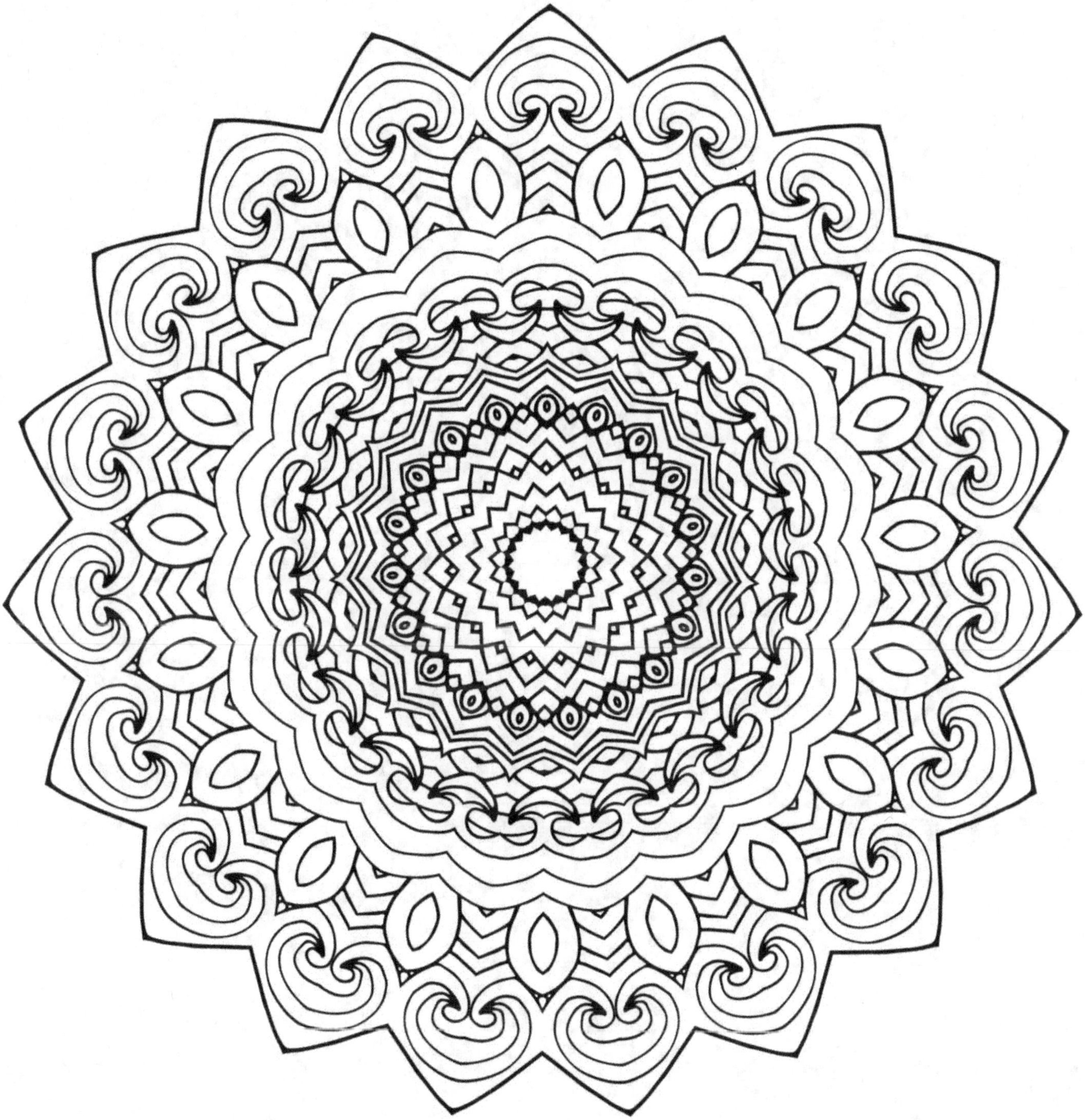

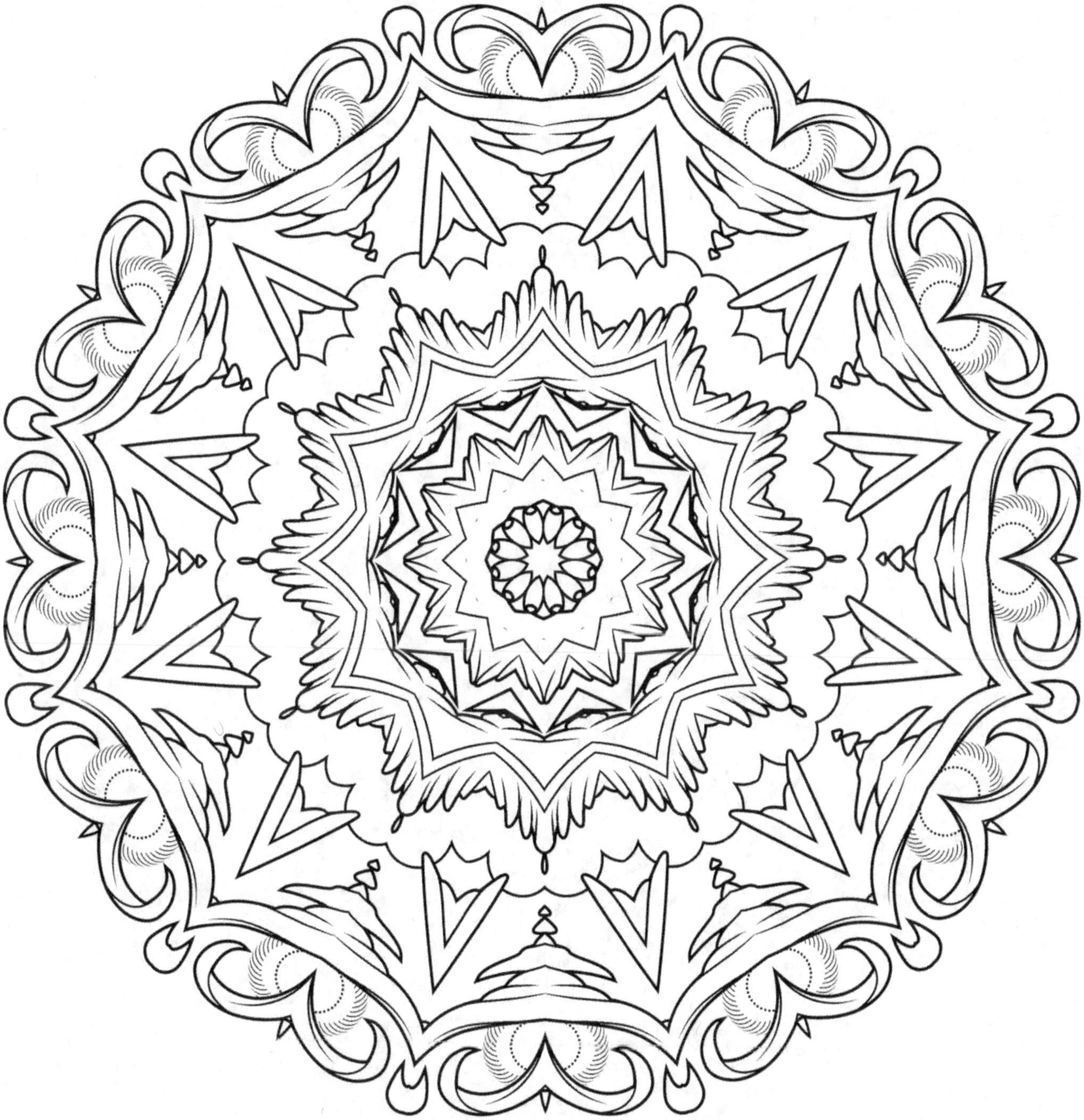

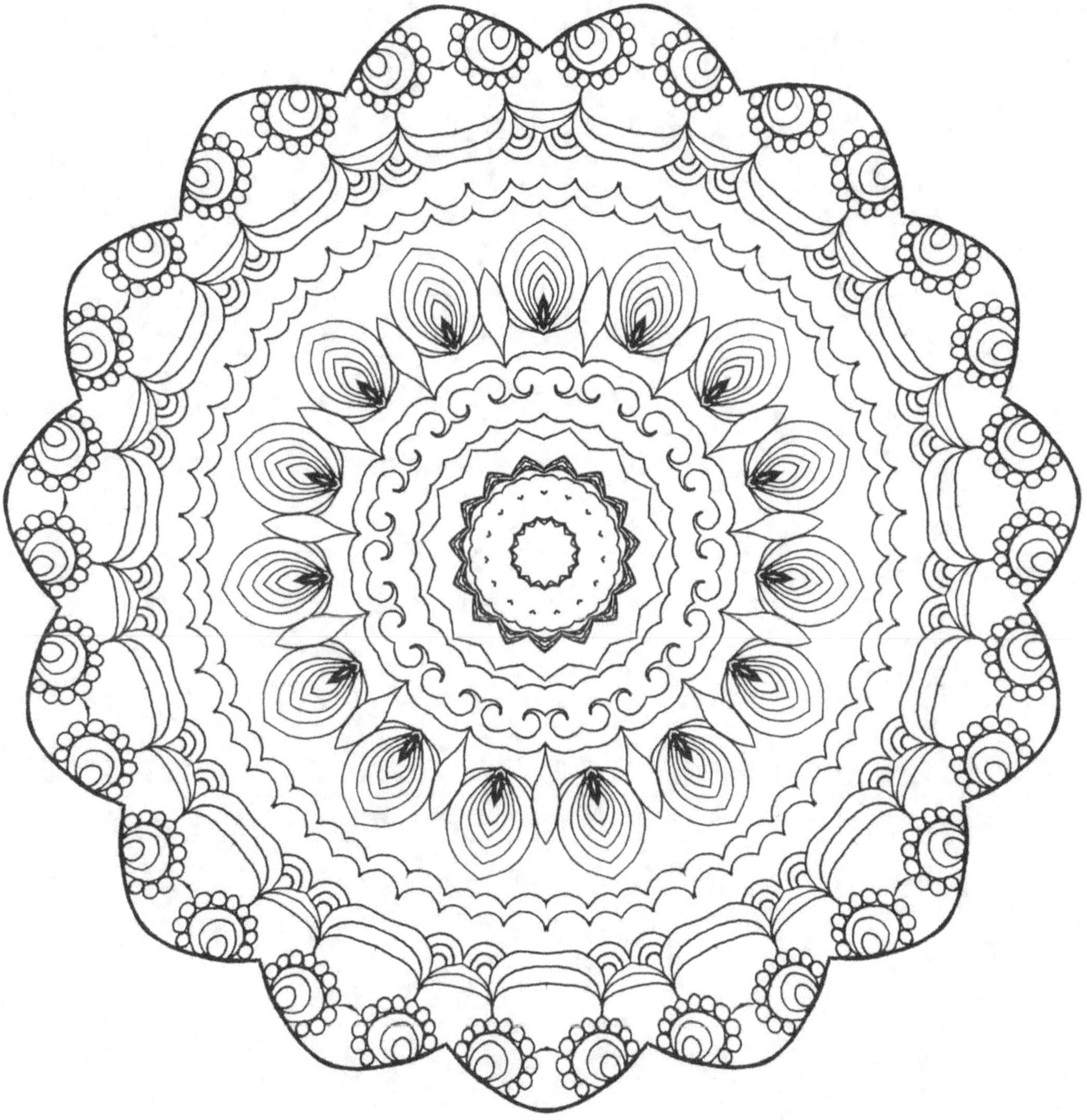

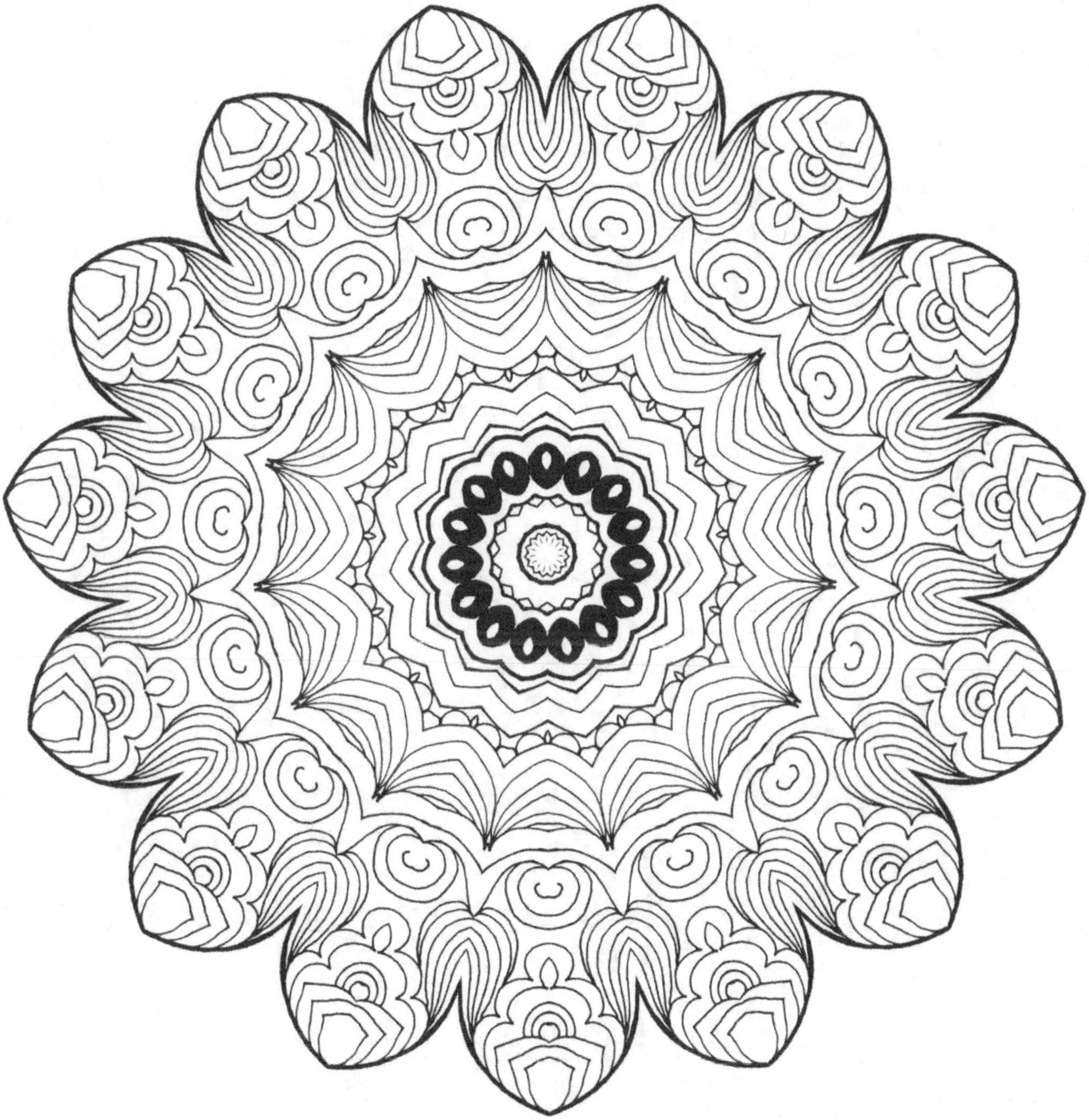

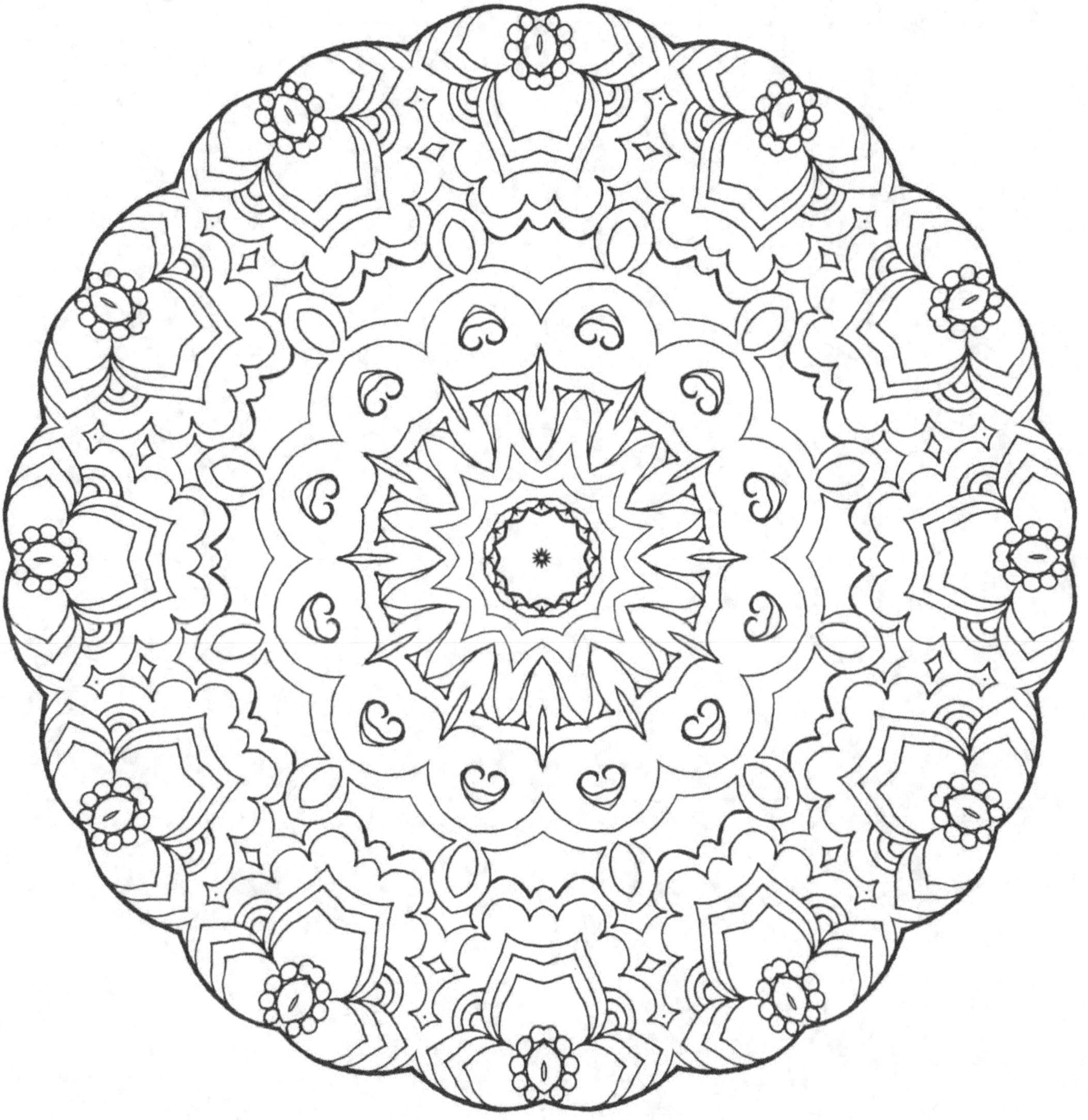

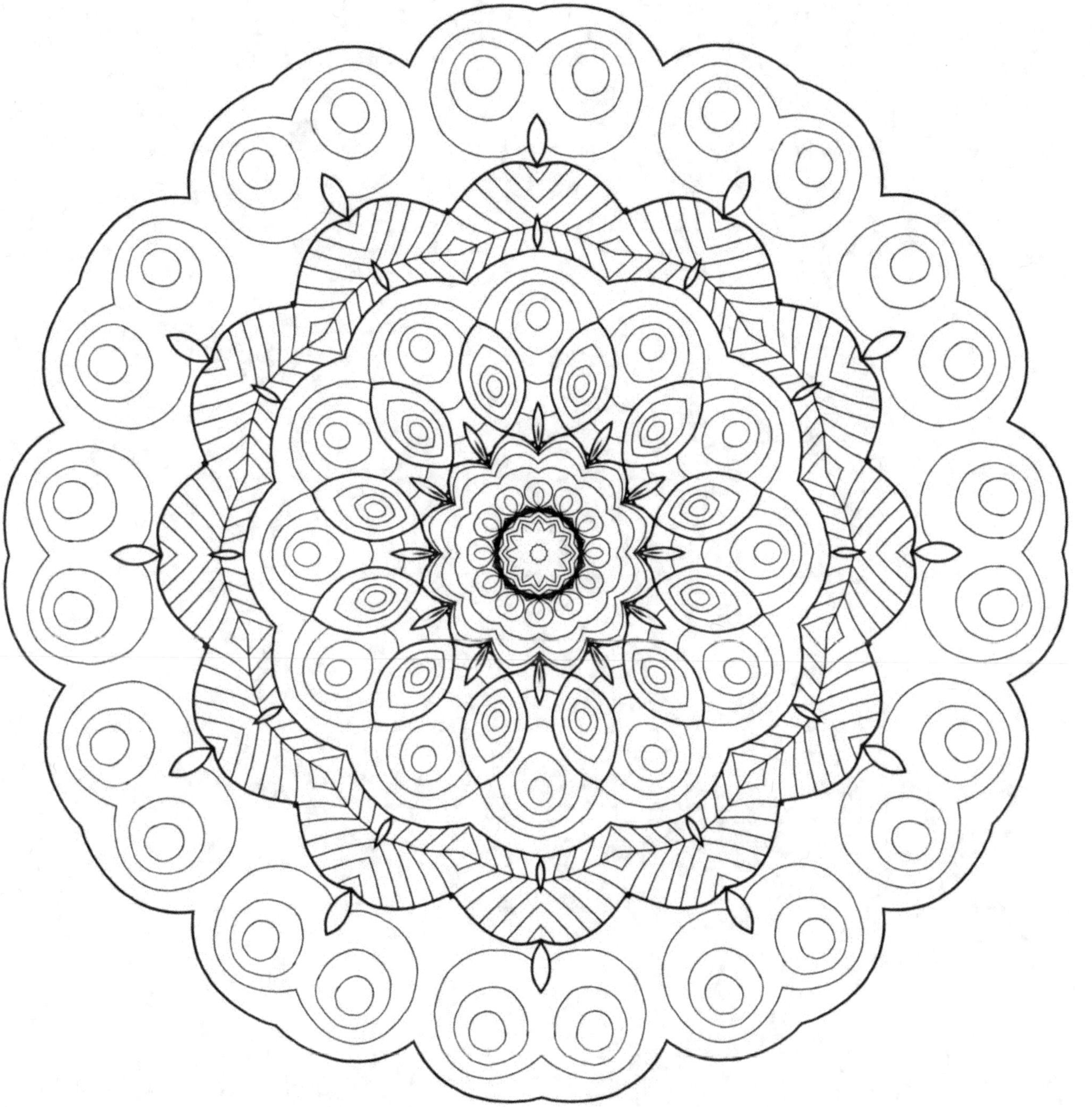

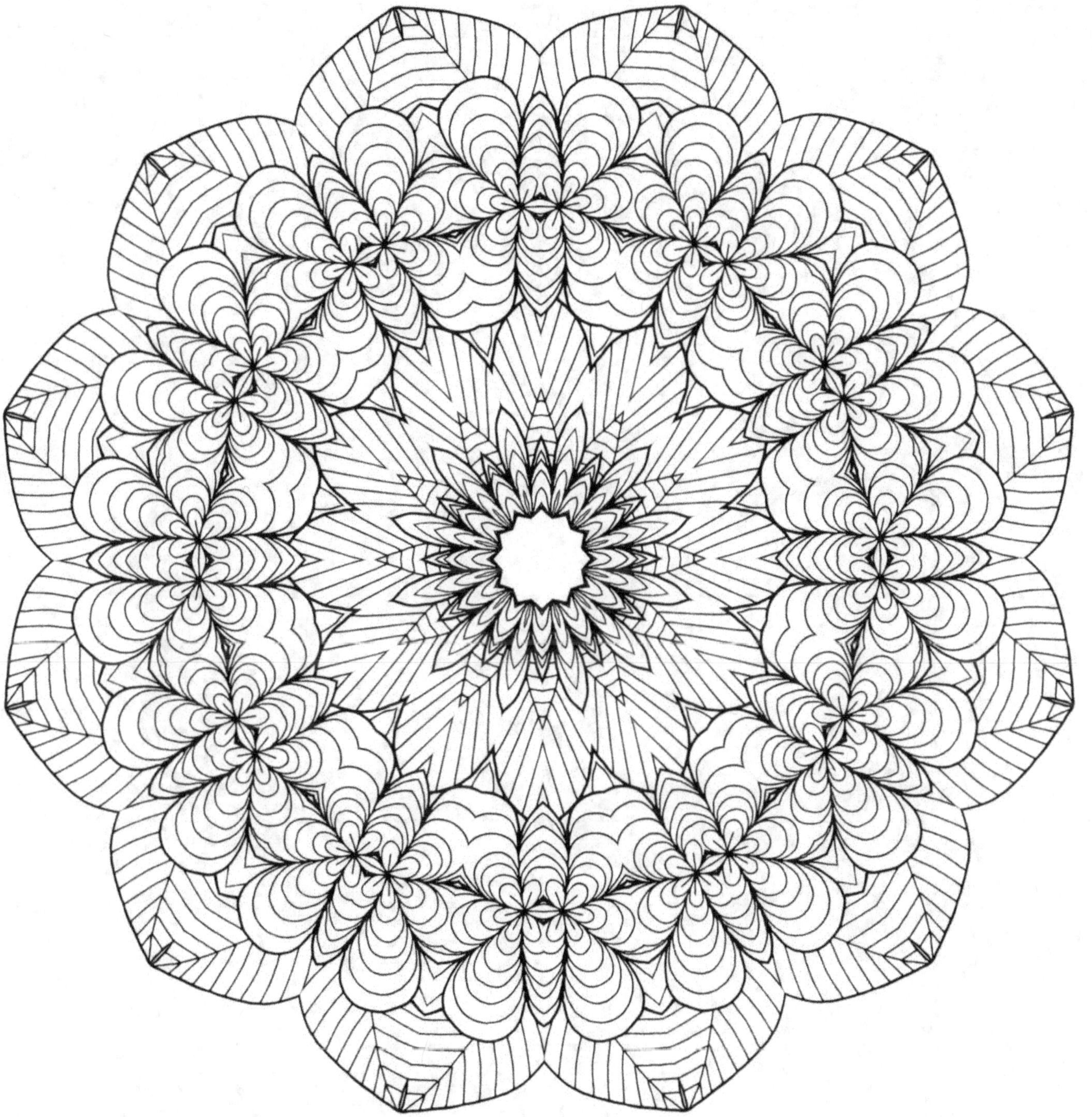

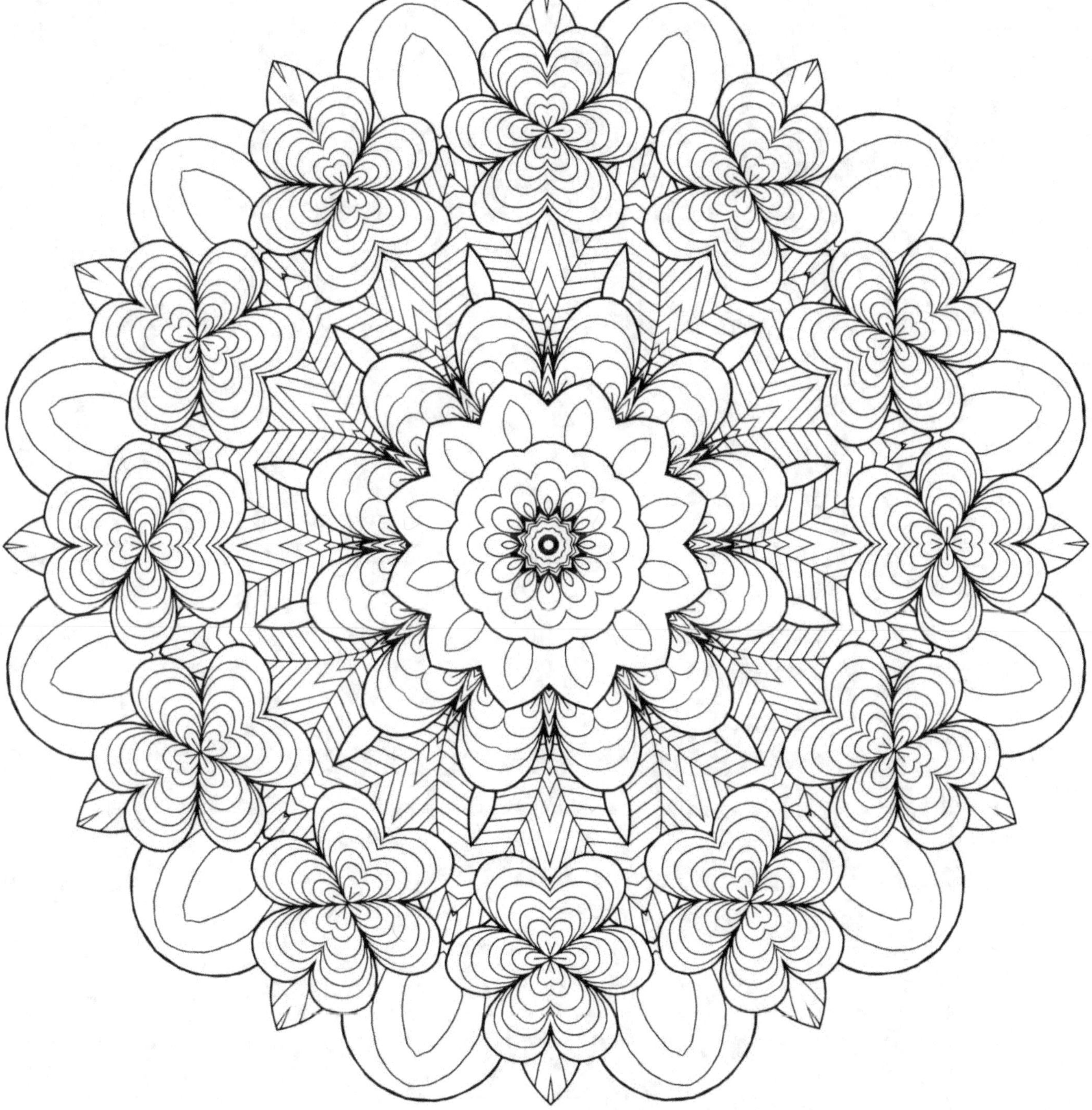

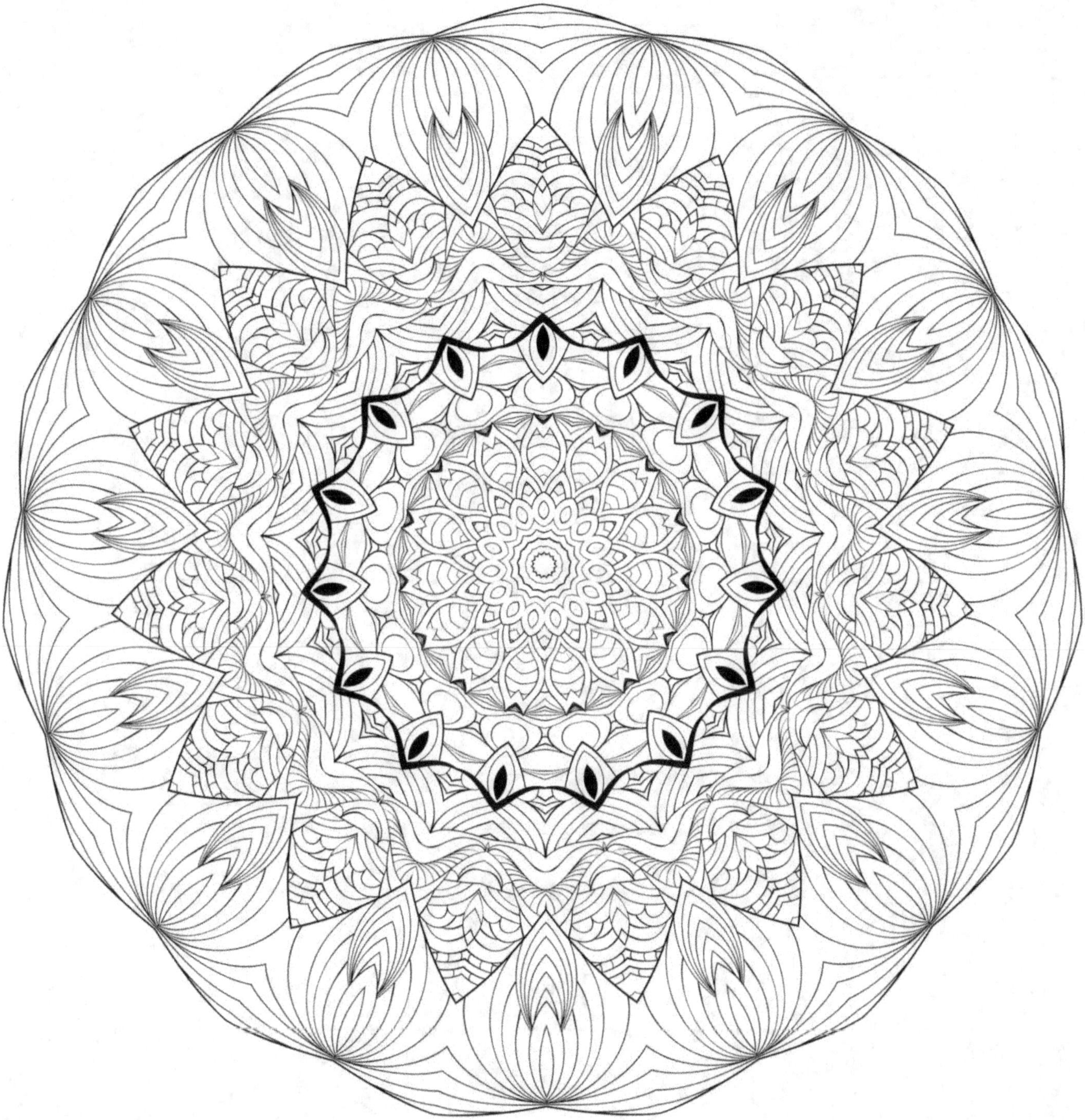

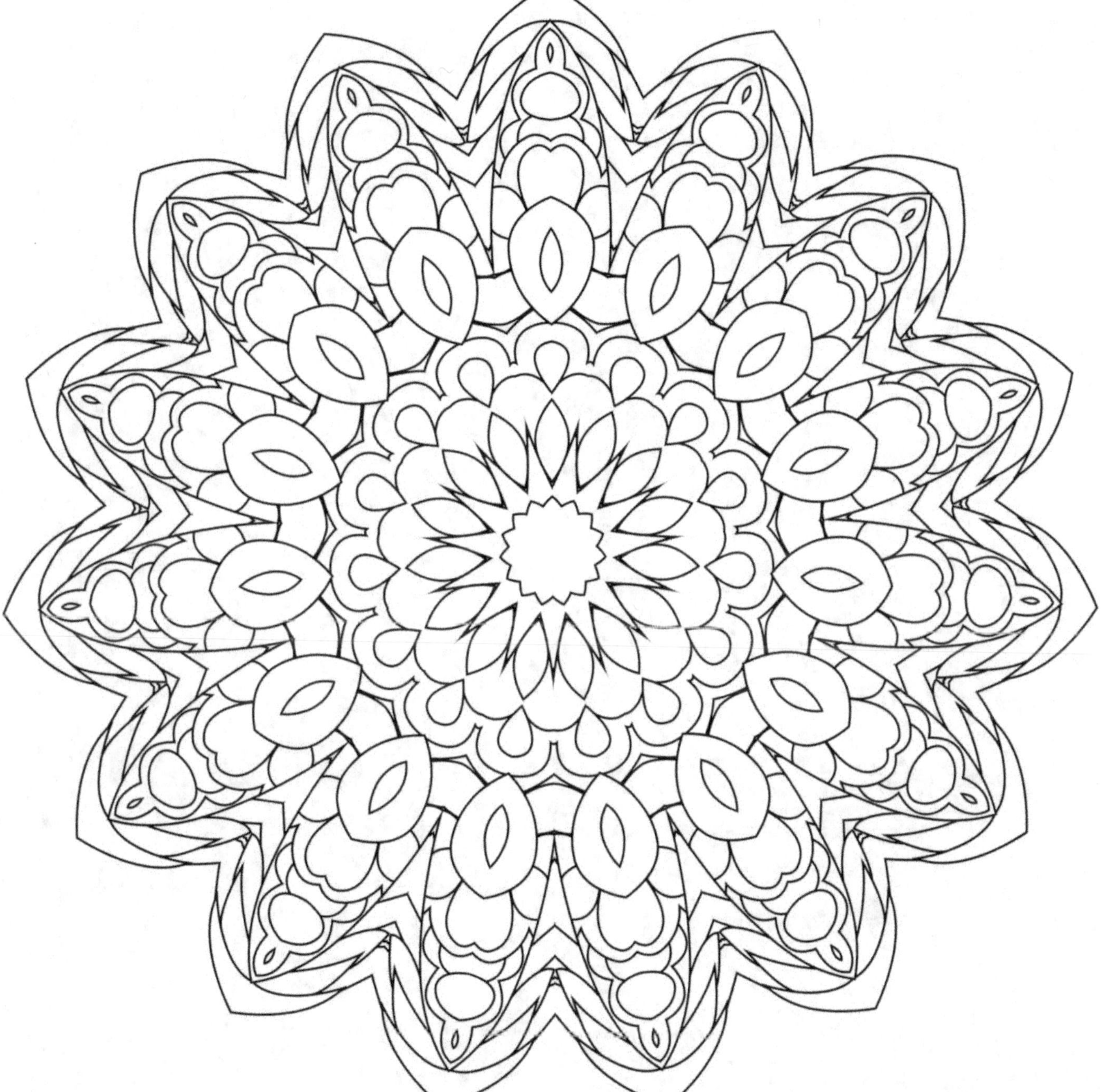

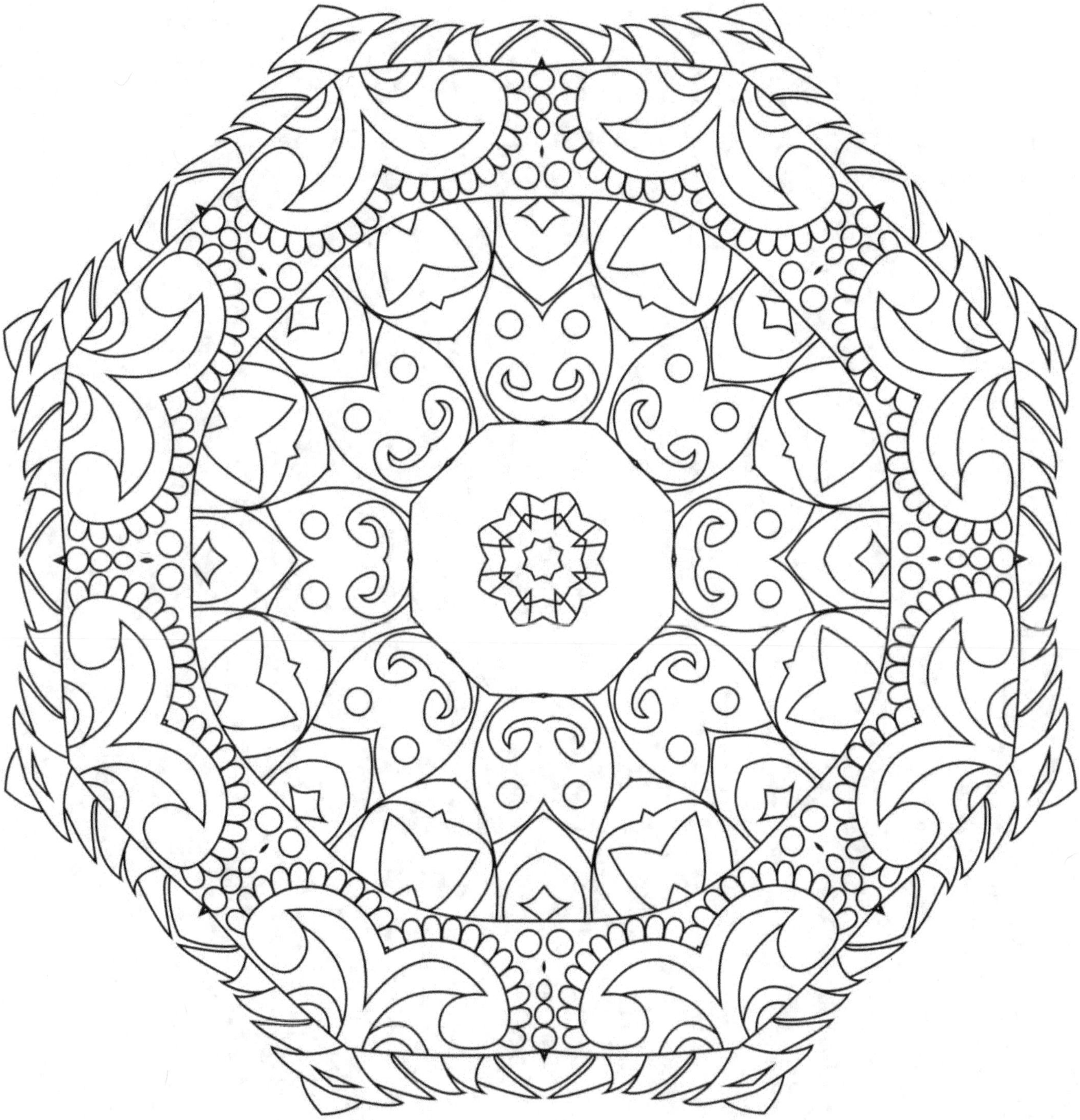

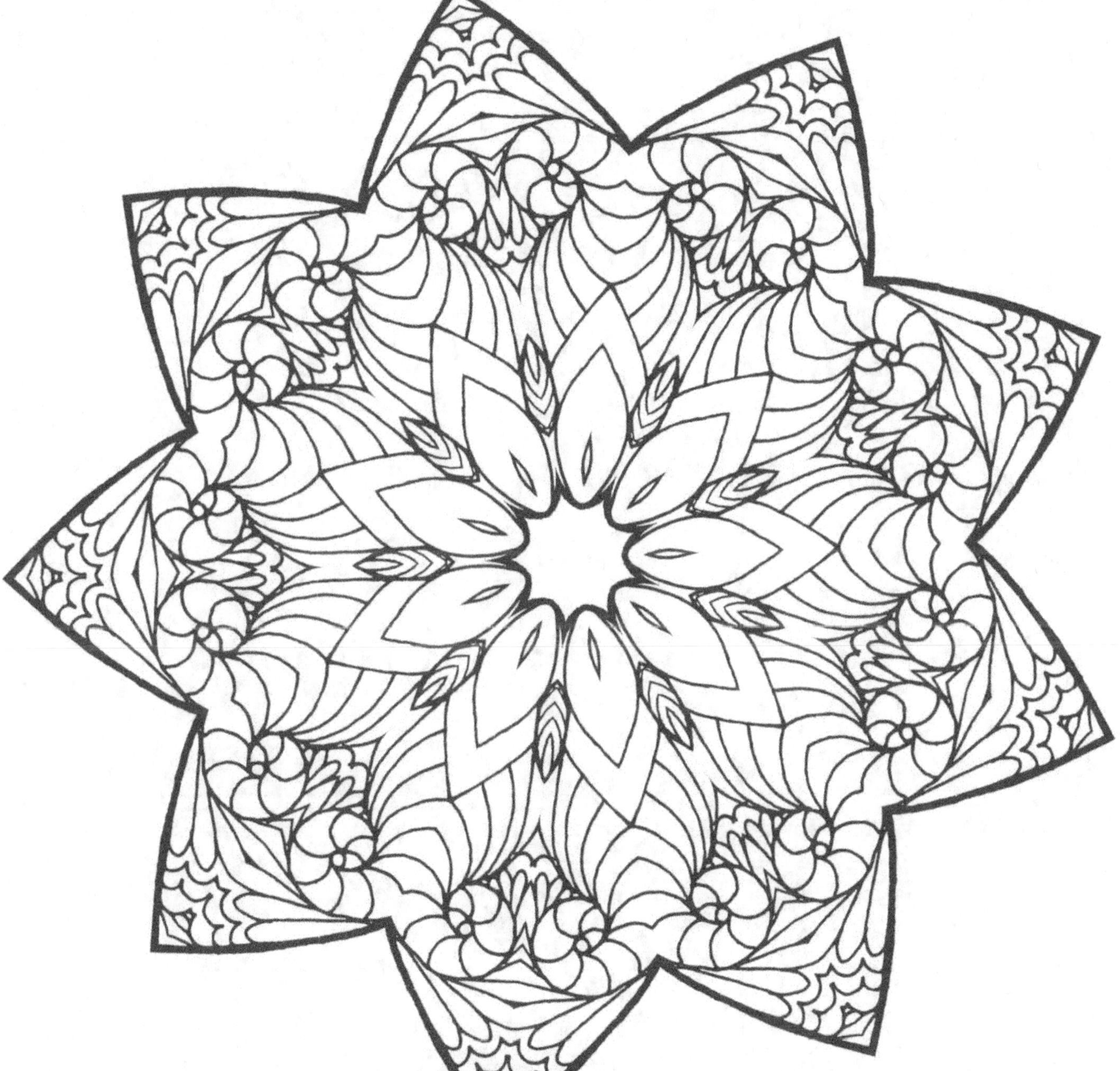

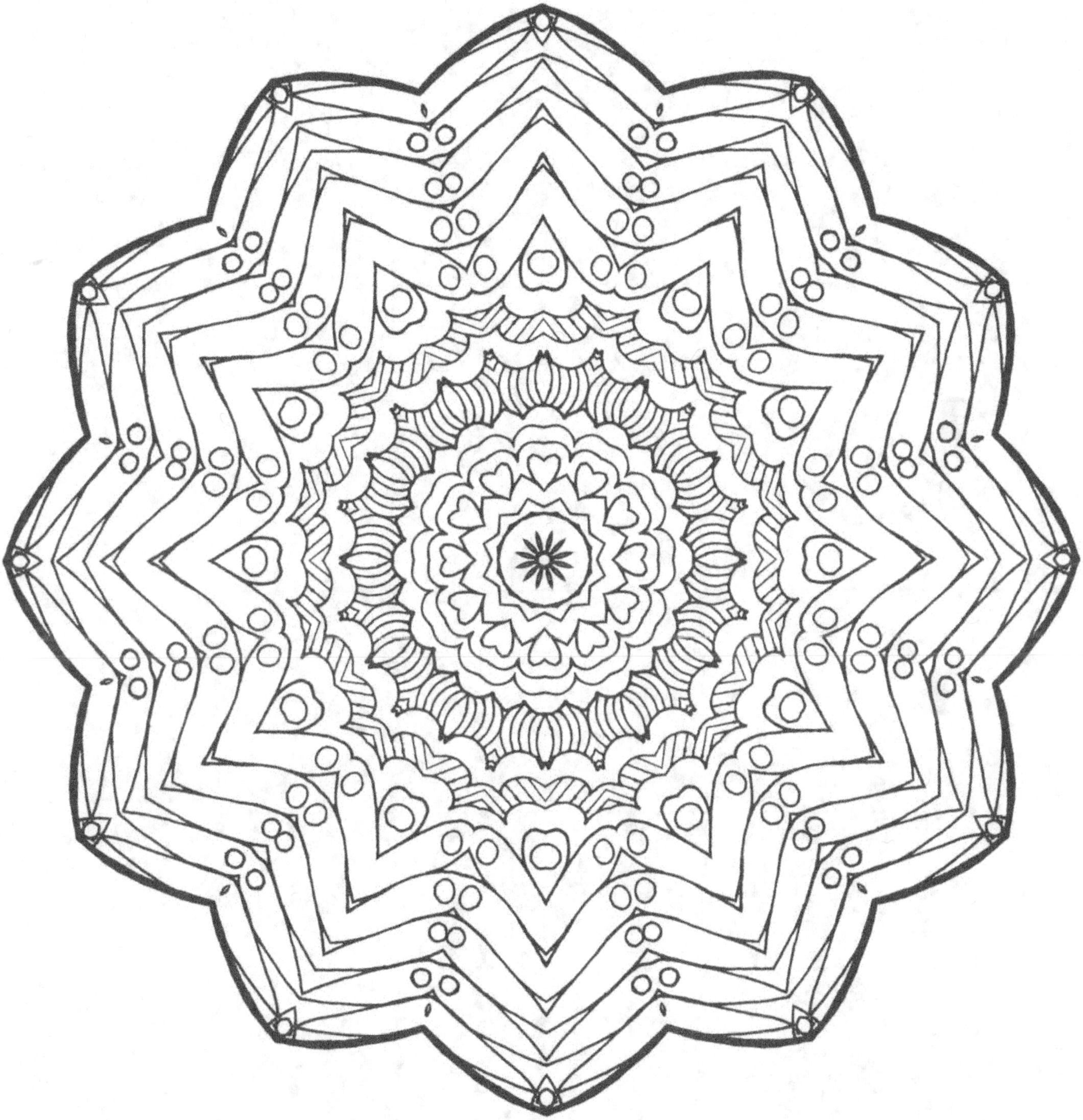

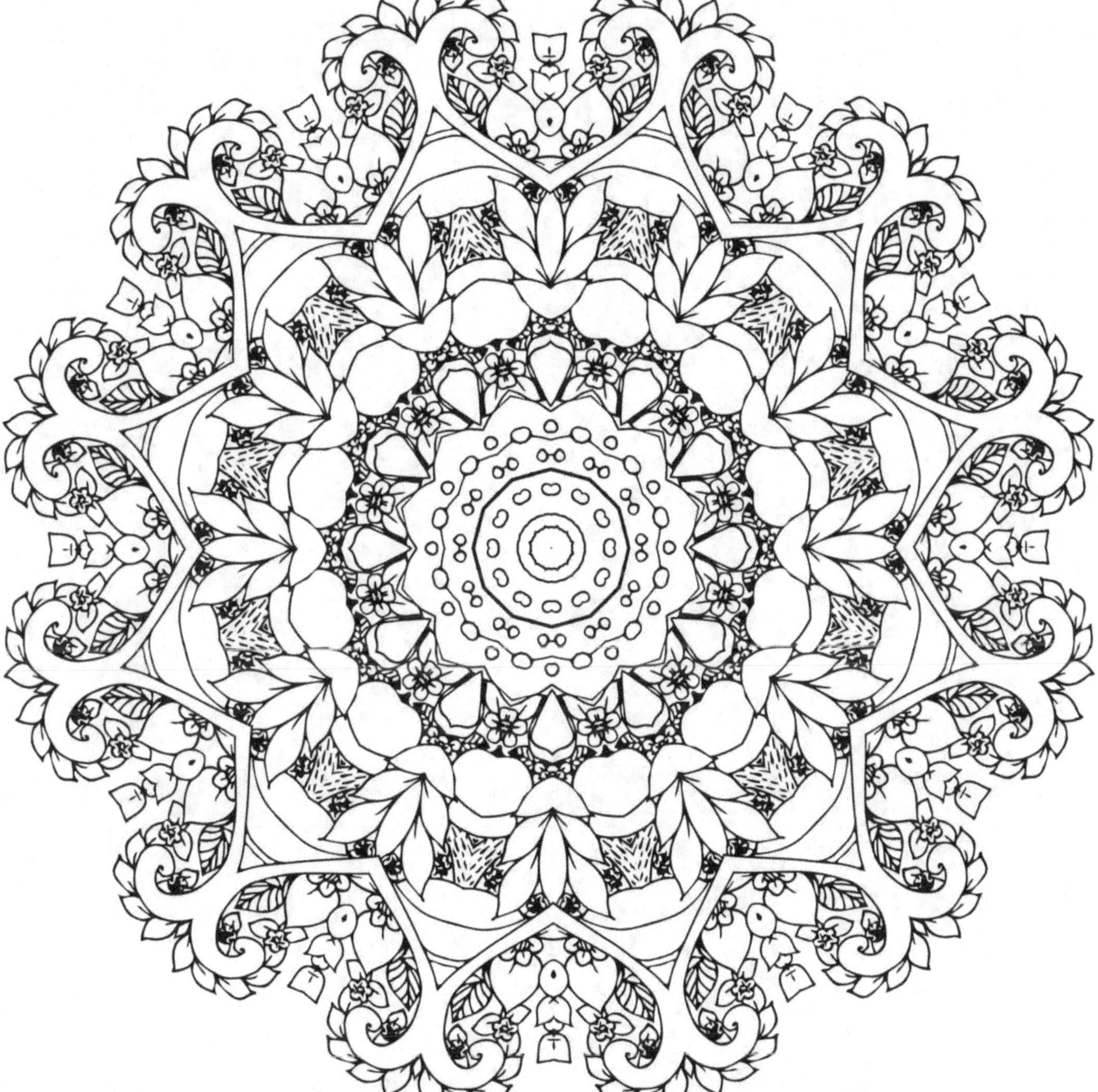

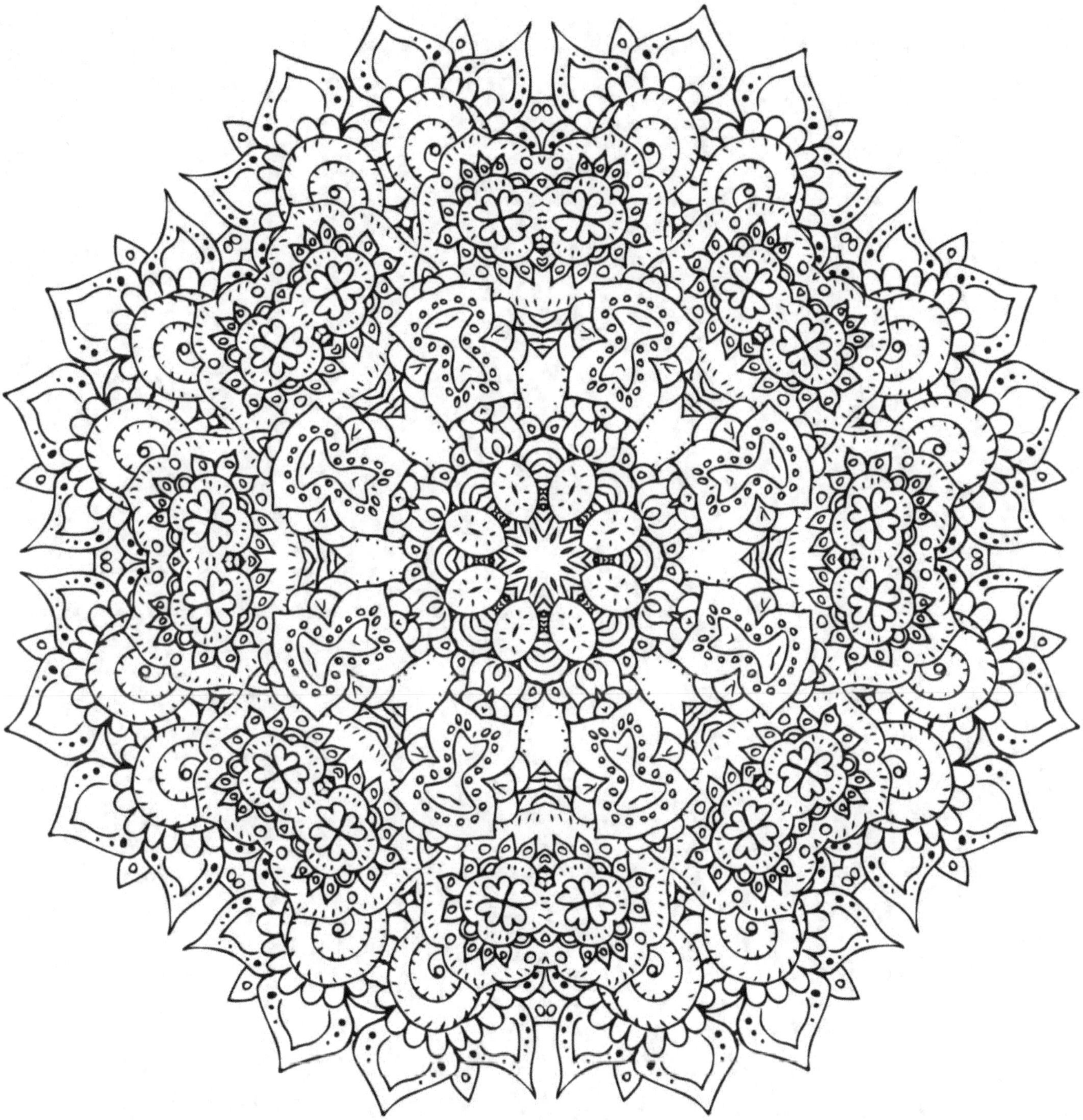

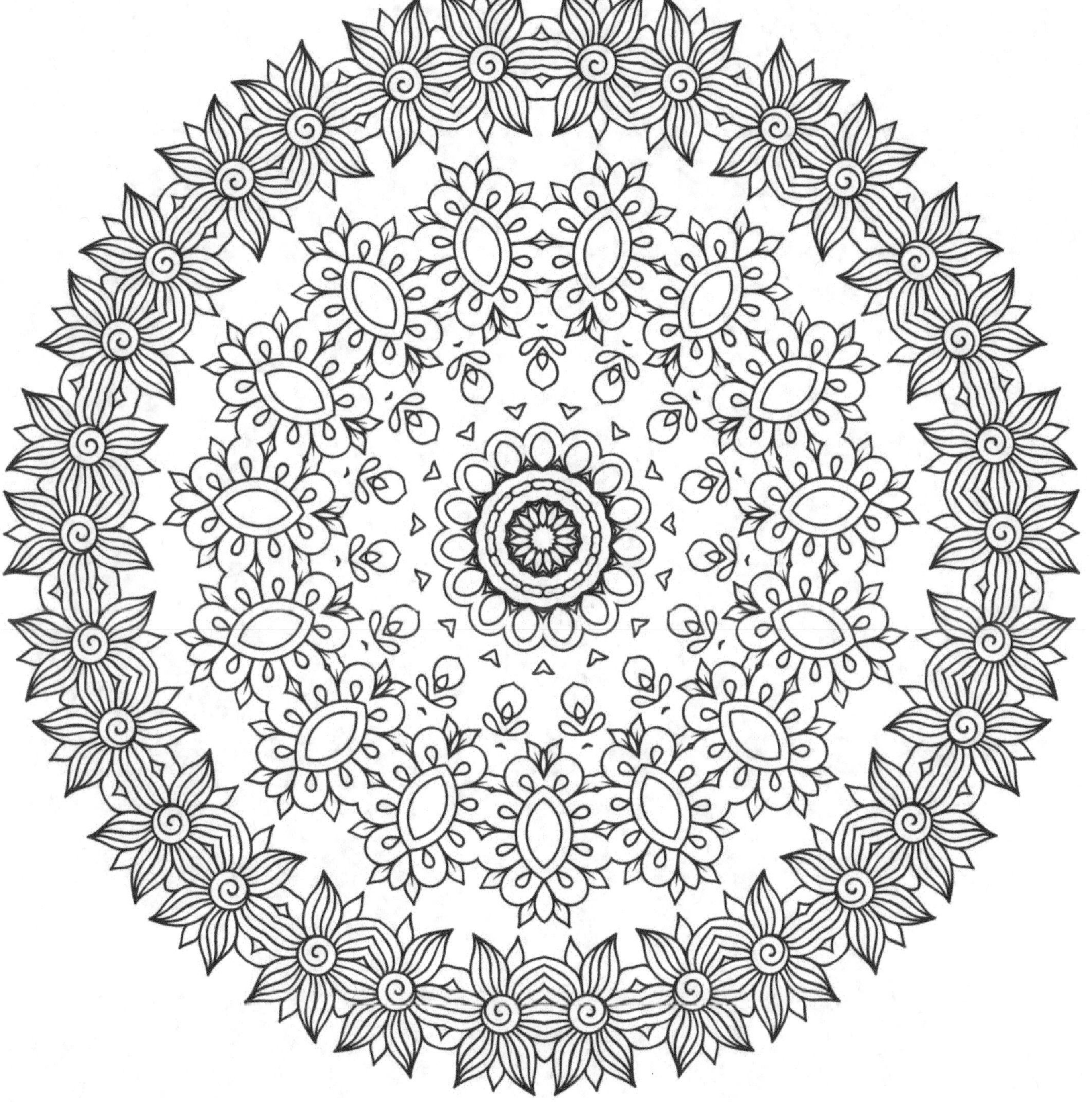

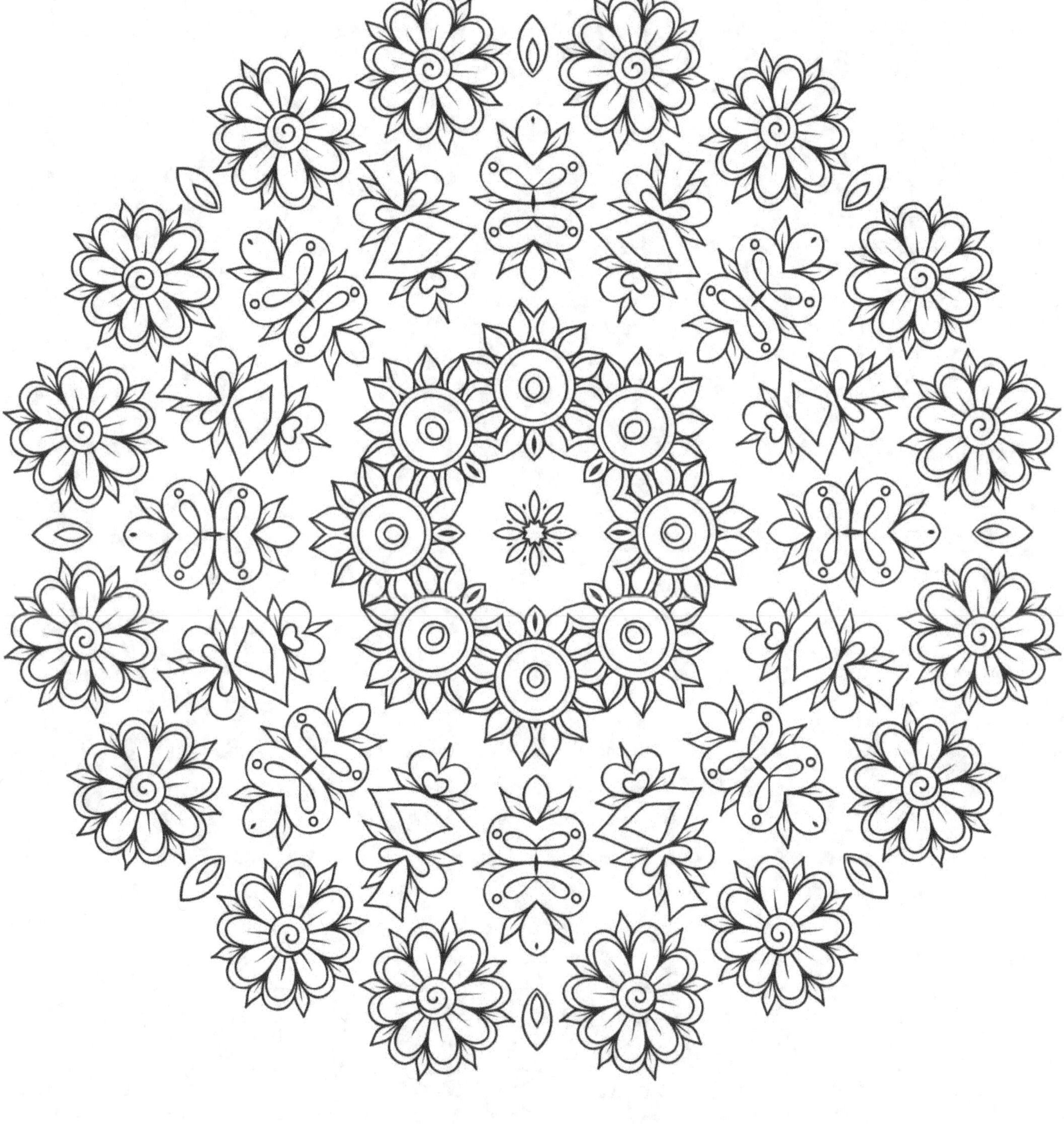

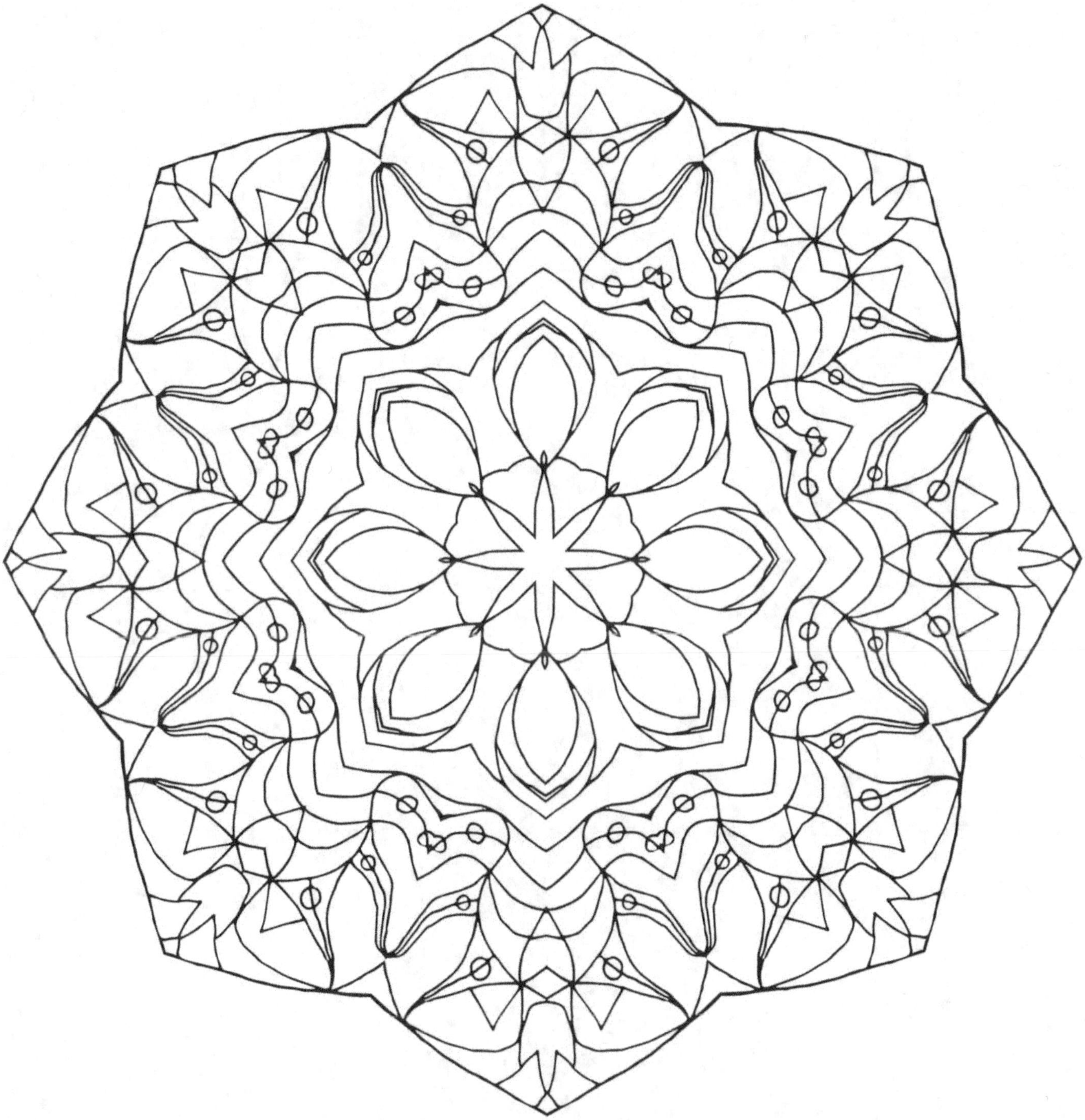

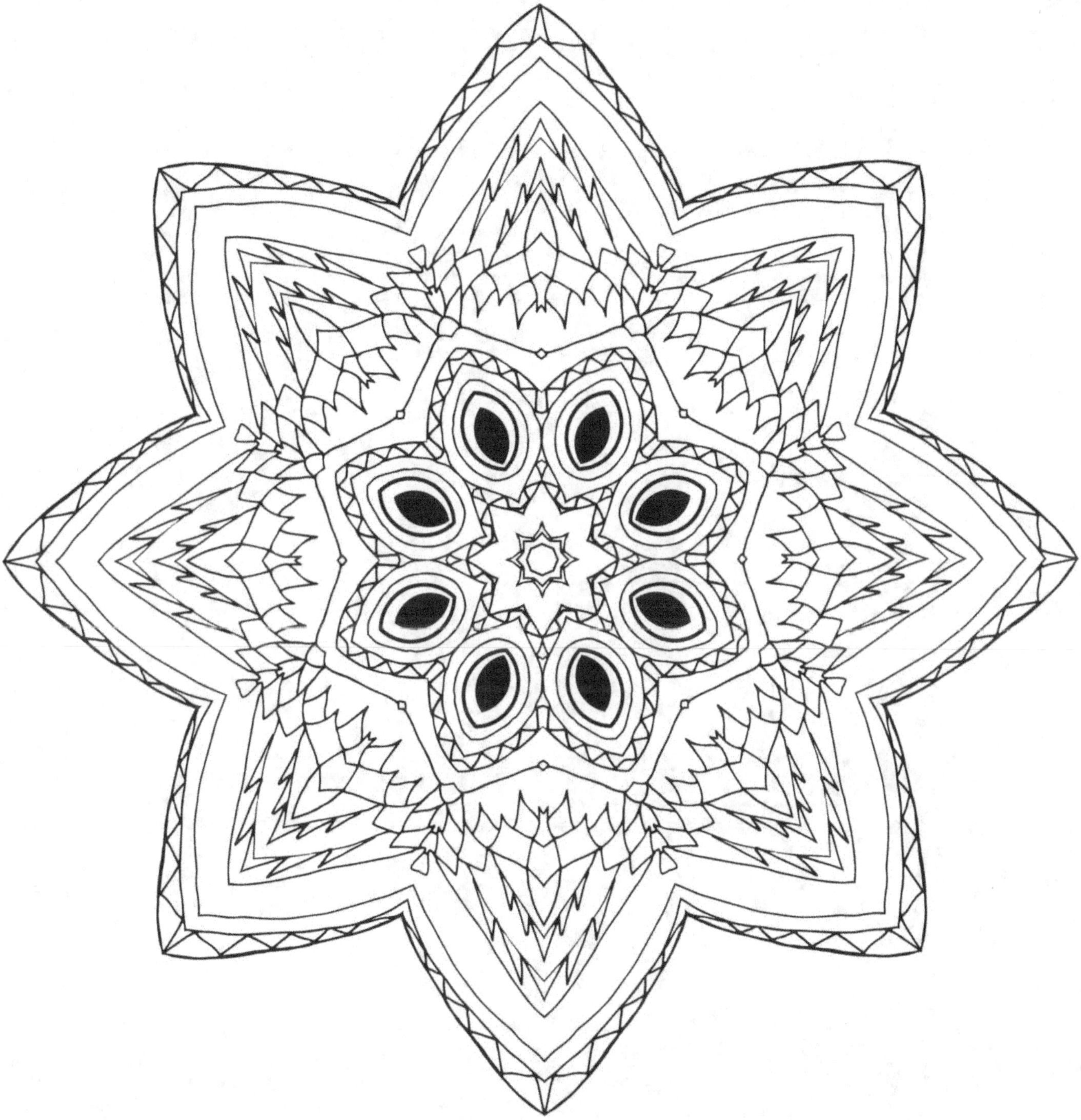

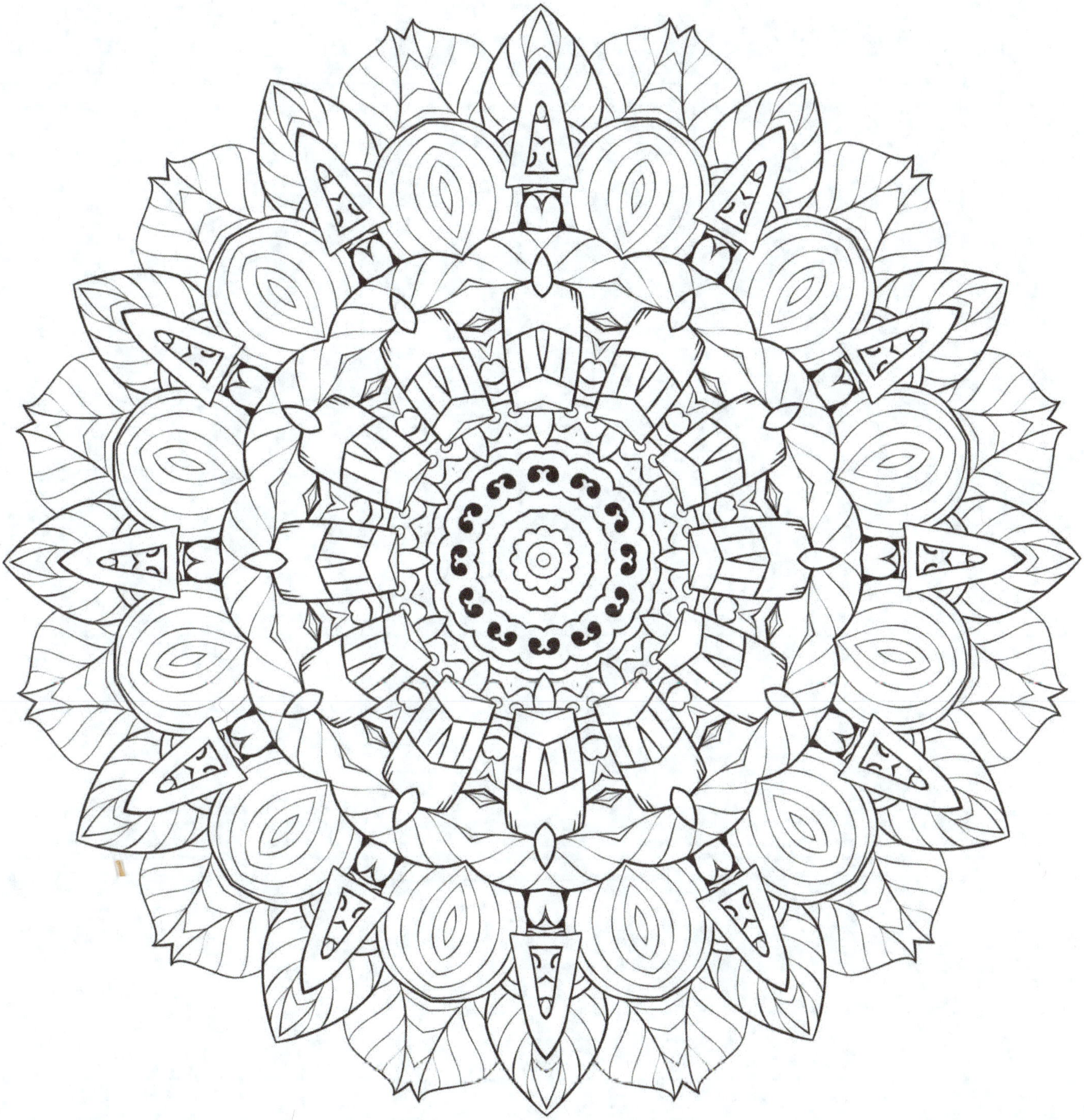

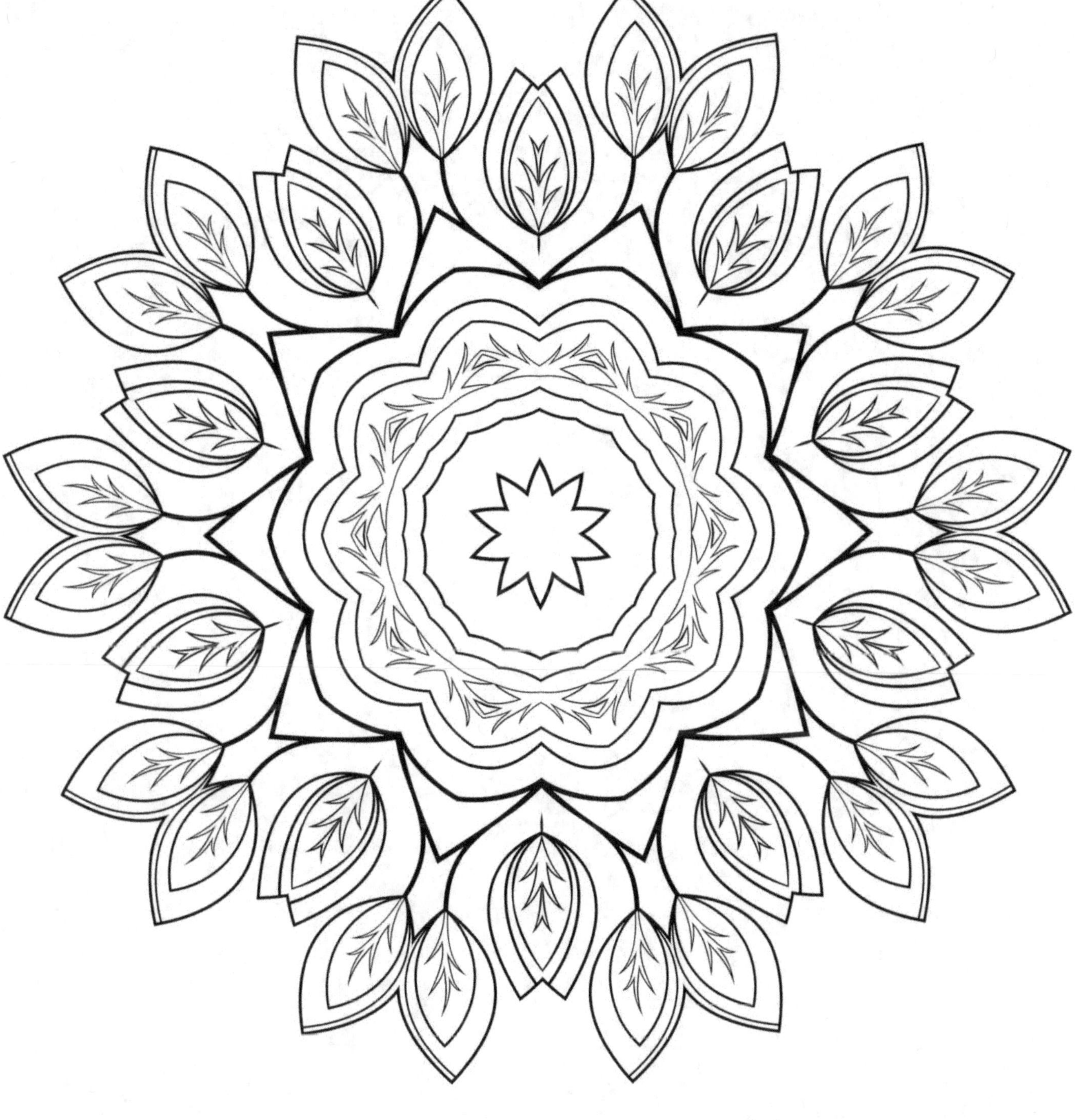

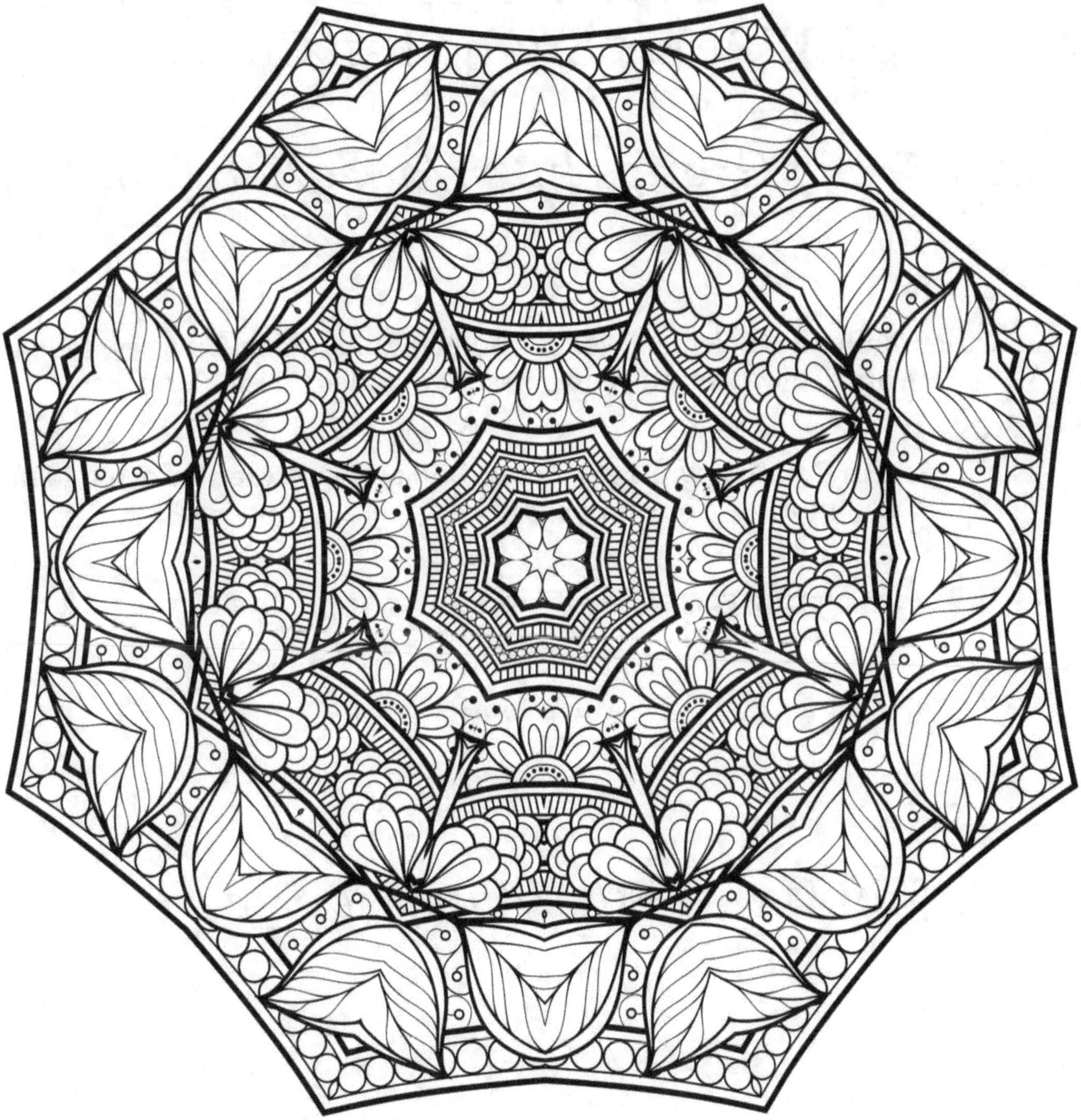

www.ingramcontent.com/pod-product-compliance
Lightning Source LLC
Chambersburg PA
CBHW082219220526
45470CB00010B/3232
* 9 7 8 1 9 7 4 5 9 8 2 8 1 *